Majestic Range Catalog and Cook Book

by

Majestic Range Company

APPLEWOOD BOOKS
Bedford, Massachusetts

Majestic Range Catalog and Cook Book

was originally published in

1893

ISBN: 978-1-4290-1115-0

Thank you for purchasing an Applewood book.
Applewood reprints America's lively classics—
books from the past that are still of interest
to the modern reader.
For a free copy of
a catalog of our
bestselling
books,
write
to us at:
Applewood Books
Box 365
Bedford, MA 01730
or visit us on the web at:
For cookbooks: foodsville.com
For our complete catalog: awb.com

Prepared for publishing by HP

MAJESTIC RANGE

CATALOGUE

AND

COOK BOOK.

HARPER, REYNOLDS & CO.,

LOS ANGELES, CAL.

INDEX.

Oh, better, no doubt, is a dinner of herbs,
When season'd by love, which no rancor disturbs;
But if, out of humor, and hungry, alone,
A man should sit down to a dinner, each one
Of the dishes of which the cook chooses to spoil
On a horrible stove, with worry and toil,
The chances are ten against one, we must own,
He gets up as ill-temper'd as when he sat down.
Indigestion, that conscience of every bad stomach,
Which relentlessly gnaws and pursues him with some ache
And trouble remorseless, and makes him heart sick,
Can be only avoided by the use of a "Majestic."

INTRODUCTION.

In placing this book before the public, we do not claim originality, the recipes being largely borrowed from "Practical Housekeeping." They have been carefully arranged with the view to being made readily, appetizingly and economically.

Bad cooking is waste of money and loss of comfort. Thousands of people are deprived of half the actual nutriment of their food because of bad cooking and the absence of means to render it palatable and digestible. With the aid of these recipes, and the food cooked in the Majestic Range, much discomfort may be saved.

One of the essentials to good cooking is to use the very best cooking apparatus. There is no economy in buying an inferior article; get the best, and let the economy be shown in the way they are used. A few dollars additional cost ought not to deter people who have the health of their families at heart from procuring the necessaries of life.

There is no article which enters more largely into our everyday life than the cooking range, and the greatest care should be taken to discriminate against those of inferior make; which may be avoided by using none but the MAJESTIC, which is made of the best selected material.

It is becoming fashionable to economize, and housekeepers are really finding it a pleasant pastime to search out and stop waste in household expense, and to exercise the thousand little economies which thoughtful and careful women understand so readily and practice with such grace.

Every young housekeeper must begin at the beginning, and blunder into a knowledge of the practical duties of a household, wasting time, temper and money in mistakes.

With the simple instructions in this pamphlet, we hope that such blunders and mistakes will not occur.

TO OUR PATRONS.

We present this, our latest Majestic Range Illustrated Catalogue and Cook-Book, with our compliments.

Our esteemed and very liberal friends will accept our thanks for their zeal and earnest co-operation in aiding and assisting in the introduction, and placing in the homes of appreciative people, such a vast number of our Majestic Ranges; and we confidently anticipate, with their continued good-will, in the year 1893 to still very largely increase the sales. Never before in the experienee of business has such a phenomenal trade in so short a time been built up. It was our aim from the inception of this enterprise, to make none but the best, and not to take from but to add to the value and efficiency of our goods, knowing that we and our customers would profit thereby.

We needed your co-operation and received it; and in return we add to your stock of wealth, the most complete line of Majestic malleable and steel ranges ever placed before a discriminating people. The entire line is new and complete, with increased size of ovens; improved pin extension water fronts for pressure boilers or open tanks; new open water heater, connecting with oblong copper reservoir, doing away with the old style of pipe connections, which fill with lime incrustations and are so liable to burst by freezing; improved fire linings; enlarged lower warming ovens; new gravity oven door handles; new process for riveting (not bolting) malleable top frames to steel body; new and complete line of Hotel Ranges in all sizes; new copper-lined Steam Tables and Carving Tables; full line of Charcoal Broilers; our Combination Broiler and Waffle Irons; Laundry Stoves for families; and this our new and exquisite one-hundred-page Illustrated Cook Book, which will accompany every range sold. To these betterments we have added a little more nickel and polish, not sufficient, however, to materially increase the labor of the user or to injure the sale of the range.

We feel that these changes and improvements, while costing us much money, will greatly facilitate sales and add popularity to the already popular "Majestic."

Anticipating your every want, and looking forward to the time when the demand will be only for "The Majestic,"

We are, as ever, yours truly,

MAJESTIC MANUFACTURING CO.

TESTIMONIALS.

Thousands of Majestic Ranges are now in the homes of as many honest purchasers, each of whom would gladly give us permission to sign their names to any kind of testimonial we might see proper to write; but we feel that the recipes for good and wholesome food are of far greater value to our friends than to fill this book with recommendations. We suggest that you see your neighbors; if they do not possess a "Majestic" advise them to buy one at once; and after a trial exchange congratulations, which will be a recommendation to other neighbors and friends. Remember, that each and every "Majestic" is guaranteed to work to perfection.

NOTE.—On the three last pages of this book will be found Majestic Range cuts lettered A, B and C respectively. They are only designed to show attachments that can be connected with any family range on preceding pages. In ordering please be governed by the number on range, and from ranges A, B or C select such extra attachments as may be desired; if Pressure Boiler or Charcoal Broiler, state which end of range to be connected, right or left. The price on hotel ranges includes double mantel shelf. Our open reservoir as shown on family sizes cannot be connected with either 55, 56, 57, 58 or 59.

MATERIAL.

The life of a range depends on quality more than on the weight of material. A range made of cast and wrought iron is heavier, but on account of its inferior character will not last half so long, as one made of malleable iron and wrought steel weighing much less. It is a well established fact, that ranges made of malleable and wrought steel and best gray iron are in every way superior to ranges made of wrought and cast iron, or of cast iron wholly. Few people understand the process of making malleable or know the enormous expense connected with its manufacture for range work, nor have we the space to go into a detailed statement. Suffice to say, years in time and very large sums of money have been spent in bringing it up to its present high state of perfection.

Majestic Ranges are made of material especially manufactured for the purpose. The steel is cold rolled, thoroughly annealed and double stretched, giving a smooth and level surface; the parts in malleable iron are fully decarbonized, making them strong, durable, and equal in tensile strength to that of wrought iron—they cannot be broken by rough usage; the gray iron is made of the best quality of pig, such as will stand the greatest amount of fire service.

In our family size ranges the parts in malleable are as follows: **Oven doors and frames, warming closet doors and frames, ash pan frames, top frames, fire doors and frames, flue and clean-out frames, back flue collars, shelf corner irons, door stakes, latch and latch catches, dampers and frames, damper rods, hooks, lugs, oven buttons, door handles and number plates.**

In hotel ranges the parts in malleable are: **Oven doors and frames, oven door stakes, shoes, door handles and catches, ash pan frames, warming closet doors and frames, flue and clean-out doors and frames, shaker, cranks and lugs.** The parts in steel: **For range body, No. 14; oven body, No. 14; oven bottom, No. 10.** In the largest sizes, two numbers heavier.

With such material, and constructed as they are, Majestic Ranges will stand the test of years of hard usage without a break or flaw.

IMPROVED WATER HEATER FOR OPEN RESERVOIR.

People who have used open reservoirs with water back and pipe connections are familiar with the annoyances occasioned by the filling and burning out and freezing and bursting of such connections; but they have not given the matter thought sufficient to understand the cause.

Water contains more or less mineral and vegetable matter, and when heated to above 212 degrees such matter is left as a deposit in pipes or water heater, which gradually fills the entire space, and there being no way of cleaning these parts burn out.

Should the water freeze in these connections, the vent from heater to reservoir is cut off, the result being the bursting or explosion of water back, sometimes with force sufficient to wreck the entire apparatus; in fact, there are instances where by these explosions people have been killed.

With our new water connection as shown on this page, these dangerous complications are fully overcome, as by its open connection with reservoir it can readily be cleaned; and there being a free open ouflet from heater to reservoir renders it absolutely safe from explosion by freezing.

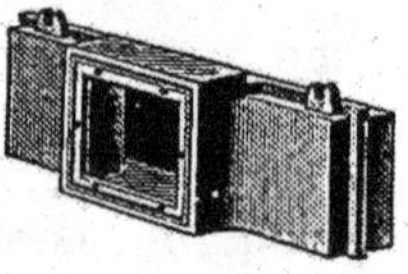

This improvement is of such importance to purchasers that they should examine carefully any cooking apparatus with reservoir connections before buying; an abundance of hot water and absolute safety should be the recommending feature.

OUR NEW PIN EXTENSION WATER FRONT.

For years the ever-present and all-important question with Range and Stove manufacturers has been, how to increase the heating surface of water backs so as to give a supply of hot water adequate for the demands, without encroaching upon the fire space or detracting from the baking qualities of the ovens,

Pipes, coils and water backs of varied and multiple forms have been devised, yet none of them can be referred to as doing the work required.

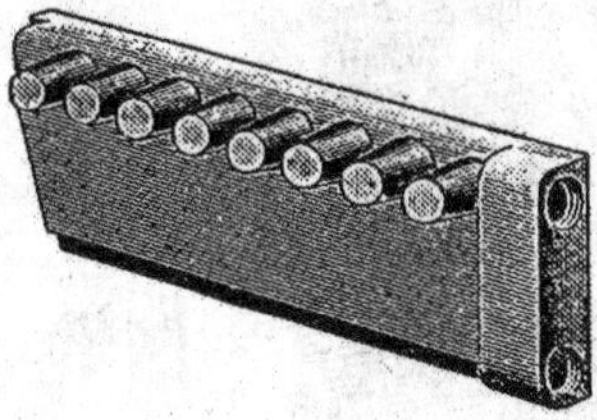

Knowing that a water back in contact with the oven chilled and destroyed its efficiency, and desiring to give the best results both in water heating and baking qualities of our ranges, we invented this new water back; and know that we have what has been so long and earnestly sought. It is inexplicable that some one before this did not study it out.

This heater, for ranges family sizes, contains 202 square inches of direct impinging fire surface; and for hotel sizes, from 225 to 262 square inches. In family ranges the heater is placed on the left side of fire box, the pins projecting into the hottest fire. In hotel ranges it can be placed on either side, as these ranges have large center flues next to fire box, hence the water backs do not affect the oven.

The accompanying cut illustrates the form and construction, and shows its wonderful capacity and heating power. Patents for this invention have been applied for.

MAJESTIC RANGE No. 37.

FOR SOFT COAL OR WOOD.

IF FOR HARD COAL OR WOOD No. 37HC.

Has no water-front. Top cooking surface 29 x 30 inches; four 8-inch lids and key-plate; oven 15 inches wide, 21 inches deep, 13 inches high; mantel shelf, large lower warming oven, bailed ash pan, heavy diagonal grates and fire-linings, protecting bar, gravity door handle and towel rod. Flue lined with pure asbestos board. Made almost entirely of malleable iron and wrought steel. It is a charming range and will do the cooking to perfection for four to six persons.

Price, $40.00.

Prices include delivery on board cars in St. Louis. Freight must be paid by purchasers—the rate varying according to distance—from 25c to $2.00 per 100 lbs.

BREAD MAKING.

The old saying, "Bread is the staff of life," has sound reason in it. Flour made from wheat, and meal from oats and Indian corn, are rich in the waste-repairing elements—starch and albumen—and head the list of articles of food for man.

Good bread makes the homeliest meal acceptable, and coarse fare appetizing, while the most luxurious table is not even tolerable without it. There is an old and true saying that "She who has baked a good batch of bread has done a good day's work."

Bread-making should stand at the head of domestic accomplishments, since the health and happiness of all depend immeasurably upon good bread; and there is certain to come a time in the experience of every true and thoughtful woman that she is glad and proud of her ability to make nice, sweet loaves, free from soda, alum and other injurious ingredients; or bitter regret that she neglected to learn, or was so unfortunate as not to have been taught at least, the first requisites of good bread-making.

Four things are indispensable to success: Good flour, good yeast, watchful care, and a Majestic Range in which to bake it.

Bread Sponge.—Six potatoes boiled on a Majestic Range and mashed, while hot, two tablespoons of white sugar, two of butter, one quart tepid water; into this stir three cups flour; beat to a smooth batter, add six tablespoons yeast; set over night, and in the morning knead in sufficient flour to make a stiff, spongy dough; knead vigorously for fifteen minutes, set away to rise, and when light knead for ten minutes; mold out into moderate-sized loaves, and let rise until they are like delicate or light sponge-cake.

Sponge for Winter Use.—Peel and boil on a Majestic Range four or five medium-sized potatoes in two quarts of water (which will boil down to one quart by the time the potatoes are cooked); when done, take out and press through a colander, or mash very fine in the crock in which the sponge is to be made; make a well in the center, into which put one cup of flour, and pour over it the boiling water from the potatoes; stir thoroughly, and when cool add a pint of tepid water, flour enough to make a thin batter, and a cup of yeast. This sponge makes very moist bread.

Good Bread.—For four small loaves boil four large potatoes; when done pour off the water, and when it cools add to it a yeast cake; mash the potato very fine, put through a sieve, pour boiling milk on as much flour as is needed, let stand until cool, add the potato and yeast, a large teaspoon of salt and one tablespoon of sugar; stir very stiff, adding flour as is needed. Let stand in a warm place until light, dissolve one teaspoon of soda in a little hot water, mix well through with the hands, mold into loaves, and let rise again. When sufficiently raised place in a moderately hot Majestic Range oven, keeping up a steady fire.

MAJESTIC RANGE No. 38.

FOR SOFT COAL OR WOOD.

IF FOR HARD COAL OR WOOD No. 38HC.

For size, construction, etc., see No. 37. The only difference being that this range is fitted with our "pin extension" water-front, as shown, ready for connection with pressure boiler, which can be attached at either end, as preferred.

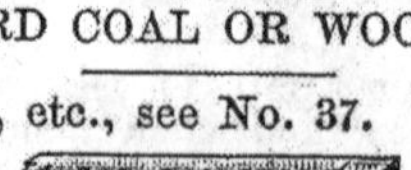

Price, $42.00.

Prices include delivery on board cars in St. Louis. Freight must be paid by purchasers—the rate varying according to distance—from 25c to $2.00 per 100 lbs.

Bread with Buttermilk.—The evening before baking, bring to the boiling point two quarts of buttermilk (or boil sour milk and take the same quantity of the whey), and pour into a crock in which a scant teacup of sifted flour has been placed. Let stand until sufficiently cool, then add half a cup of yeast, and flour to make a thick batter; the better and longer the sponge is stirred the whiter will be the bread. In the morning sift the flour into the bread-pan, pour the sponge in the center, stir in some of the flour, and let stand until after breakfast; then mix, kneading for about half an hour—the longer the better; when light, mold into loaves, this time kneading as little as possible. The secret of good bread is having good yeast and not baking too hard. This makes four loaves and forty biscuit. Bake in a Majestic Range.

Hop-Yeast Bread.—One teacup yeast, three pints warm water; make a thin sponge at tea time, cover and let it remain two hours or until very light. By adding the water to the flour first and having the sponge quite warm it is never necessary to put the sponge over hot water or in an oven to make it rise. Knead into a loaf before going to bed; in the morning mold into three loaves, spreading a little lard between as they are put in the pan. When light, bake in a Majestic Range one hour, having oven quite hot when the bread is put in, and very moderate when it is done. (Bread made in this way is never sour or heavy.) To have fine, light biscuit, add shortening at night, and in the morning make into biscuit and bake for breakfast. By this recipe bread is baked before the range is cold from breakfast, and out of the way for other baking.

To cool bread there should be a board for the purpose. An oaken board covered with heavy white flannel is the best; over this spread a fresh linen bread-cloth, and lay the bread on it right side up, with nothing over it except a very thin cover to keep off the flies. It should be placed immediately in the fresh air or wind to cool; when cool, place immediately in a tin box or stone jar, and cover closely. Bread cooled in this way will have a soft crust and be filled with pure air.

Poor-Man's Bread.—One pint of buttermilk or sour milk, one level teaspoon soda, a pinch of salt, and flour enough to make as stiff as soda-biscuit dough; cut into three pieces, handle as little as possible, roll an inch thick, place in dripping-pan, bake in a Majestic Range twenty or thirty minutes in a hot oven, and, when done, wrap in a bread-cloth. Eat while warm, breaking open like a biscuit. Each cake will be about the size of a pie.

Bread with Mush.—Pour two quarts hot corn meal mush, made as for eating, over two quarts flour (wheat or graham); when cool add one quart sponge, one coffee cup molasses, one teaspoon salt, half teaspoon soda; mix well together; add more flour if needed, and knead thoroughly; mold into small loaves; let rise and bake in small dripping pans (a loaf in a pan), or pie tins, in a Majestic Range in a moderate oven; when done rub over with butter, place on the side, wrap in a cloth, and when cold put in a jar or box. This recipe makes three good-sized loaves and keeps moist longer than all graham bread.

MAJESTIC RANGE No. 39.

FOR SOFT COAL OR WOOD.

IF FOR HARD COAL OR WOOD No. 39HC.

The top cooking surface, size of oven, and general constructive features are the same as in No. 37. The change in the number is made by reason of our 15-gallon reservoir, connected with open water heater, as shown. This reservoir is made of 16-oz. cold rolled planished copper, tinned inside, with handsome enameled and hinged cover.

Price, $51.00.

Salt-Rising Bread.—The leaven for this bread is prepared thus: Take a pint of warm water—about ninety degrees (if a little too hot defeat is certain)—in a perfectly clean bowl and stir up a thick batter, adding only a teaspoon of salt; a thorough beating of the batter is important. Set in a pan of warm water to secure uniformity of temperature, and in two to four hours it will begin to rise. The rising is much more sure if coarse flour or "shorts" is used instead of fine flour.

When your "rising" is nearly light enough, take a pint of milk and a pint of boiling water (a tablespoon of lime water added is good and often prevents souring); mix the sponge in the bread-pan, and when cooled to about milk-warm stir in the rising. The sponge thus made will be light in two to four hours, with good warmth. The dough requires less kneading than yeast-raised dough. The bread is simpler, but not so certain of rising, and you leave out all the ingredients save the flour, water (milk is not essential), and a pinch of salt. It should be made more frequently as it dries faster than bread containing potatoes. Some object to it because of the odor in rising, which is the result of acetous fermentation, but the more of that the more sure you are having sweet bread when baked. Bake in a Majestic Range.

Brown Bread.—Two and one-half cups sour milk, and one-half cup molasses; into these put one heaping teaspoon soda, two cups corn meal, one cup graham flour and one teaspoon salt. Use coffee cups. Steam three hours, and afterwards brown in a Majestic Range oven.

Boston Brown Bread.—One heaping coffee cup each of corn, rye and graham meal. The rye meal should be as fine as the graham, or rye flour may be used. Sift the three kinds together as closely as possible, and beat together thoroughly with two cups of New Orleans or Port Rico molasses, two cups sweet milk, one cup sour milk, one dessertspoon soda, one teaspoon salt; pour into a tin form, place in a kettle of cold water, put on a Majestic Range and boil four hours. Put on to cook as soon as mixed. It may appear to be too thin, but it is not, as this recipe has never been known to fail. Serve warm, with baked beans or Thanksgiving turkey. The bread should not quite fill the form (or a tin pail with cover will answer), as it must have room to swell. See that the water does not boil up to the top of the form; also take care that it does not boil entirely away or stop boiling. To serve it, remove the lid and set it a few moments into the open oven to dry the top, and it will then turn out in perfect shape. This bread can be used as a pudding, and served with a sauce made of thick sour cream, well sweetened and seasoned with nutmeg; or it is good toasted the next day.

Eastern Brown Bread.—One pint each of rye or graham and Indian meal, one cup molasses, three-fourths cup sour milk, one and one-half teaspoons soda, one and one-half pints cold water. Put on range over cold water (all brown breads are better when put on to steam over cold water, which is afterwards brought to the boiling point and kept constantly boiling until bread is done); steam four hours, and brown over in the Majestic Range oven.

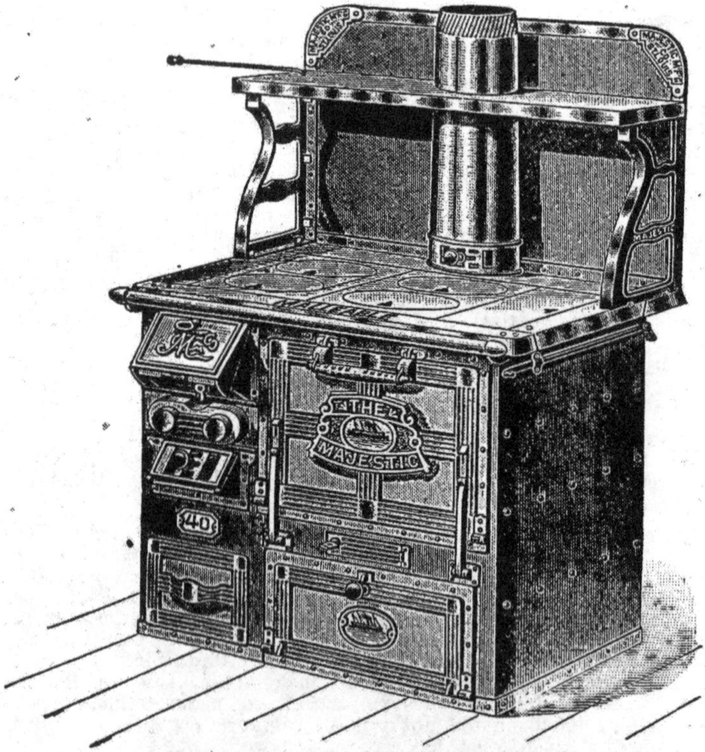

MAJESTIC RANGE No. 40.

FOR SOFT COAL OR WOOD.

IF FOR HARD COAL OR WOOD No. 40HC.

Has no water-front. Top cooking surface 29 x 33 inches; four 8-inch lids and wide key-plate; oven 17 inches wide, 21 inches deep, 13 inches high; mantel shelf, large lower warming oven, bailed ash pan, heavy diagonal grates and fire-linings, protecting bar, gravity door handle and towel rod. Flue lined with pure asbestos board. Made almost entirely of malleable iron and wrought steel. It is symmetrical and beautiful in proportions, and will do the cooking for six to eight persons.

Price, $43.00.

Prices include delivery on board cars in St. Louis. Freight must be paid by purchasers—the rate varying according to distance—from 25c to $2.00 per 100 lbs.

Bread, in Summer or Winter.—In summer take three pints of cold or tepid water, four tablespoons of yeast, one teaspoon of salt; stir in flour enough to make a thick sponge (rather thicker than griddle-cakes). Let stand until morning, then add more flour, mix stiff, and knead ten minutes; place in a pan, let rise until light, knead for another ten minutes; mold into four loaves and set to rise, but do not let it get too light. Bake in a Majestic Range in a moderate oven one hour. If bread is mixed at six o'clock in the morning the baking ought to be done by ten o'clock.

In winter take one pint of buttermilk or clabbered milk; let it scald (not boil); make a well in the center of the flour; into it turn the hot milk, add one teaspoon of salt, enough flour and water to make sufficient sponge, and one teacup of yeast; let stand until morning, and then prepare the bread as in summer. This is more covenient to make in winter, since a hot fire is needed to heat the milk.

Corn Bread.—One pint corn meal sifted, one pint flour, one pint sour milk, two eggs beaten light, one-half cup sugar, piece of butter size of an egg; add, the last thing, one teaspoon soda in a little milk; add to beaten egg the milk and meal alternately, then the butter and sugar. If sweet milk is used, add one teaspoon cream tartar; bake twenty minutes in a hot oven in a Majestic Range.

Corn Bread.—Take one quart buttermilk, and one heaping pint corn meal, one teaspoon soda, one of salt, one tablespoon sugar and three eggs; have the range very hot, and do not bake in too deep a pan. The batter seems too thin, but bakes very nicely in a Majestic Range.

Plain Corn Bread.—One well-heaped pint corn meal, one pint sour or buttermilk, one egg, one teaspoon soda, one of salt; bake in dripping or gem pans in a Majestic Range. If preferred, one heaping tablespoon of sugar may be added.

Graham Bread.—Mix three quarts Graham flour, one quart warm water, half pint yeast, a quarter pint molasses, and one tablespoon salt thoroughly; put in well-buttered pans, and leave in a warm place to rise, or let it rise over night at 60°. If left to rise slowly, let it remain in the bowl in which it was mixed, and unless very light when put in pans let it stand fifteen or twenty minutes before putting in the oven. Bake in a Majestic Range.

Graham Bread.—To one and a half pints of tepid water add one heaping teaspoon of salt and one-half cup of sugar; stir in one-half pint or more of the sponge made of white flour, as in recipe for "Bread with Potato Yeast;" add Graham flour until almost too stiff to stir; put in the baking-pan and let rise well, which will take about two hours; bake in a Majestic Range in a moderate oven, and when done wrap in a wet towel until cool.

Quick Graham Bread.—One and a half pints sour milk, half cup New Orleans molasses, a little salt, two teaspoons soda dissolved in a little hot water, and as much Graham flour as can be stirred in with a spoon; pour in well-greased pan, put in oven as soon as mixed, and bake two hours in a Majestic Range.

MAJESTIC RANGE No. 41.

FOR SOFT COAL OR WOOD.

IF FOR HARD COAL OR WOOD No. 41HC.

Is an exact counterpart of No. 40, with our "pin extension" waterfront. This heater if connected to a 40-gallon pressure boiler will supply all the hot water demanded. People before purchasing a range wish to know that it is honest, effective, durable, and reasonable in price; and for these qualities we recommend it.

Price, $45.00.

Rye and Indian Bread.—One quart of rye meal or rye flour, two quarts of Indian meal, scalded (by placing in a pan and pouring just enough boiling water over it, stirring constantly with a spoon, to merely wet it, but not enough to make it into a batter), one-half teacup molasses, two teaspoons salt, one of soda, one teacup yeast; make as stiff as can be stirred with a spoon, mixing with warm water, and let rise all night; then put in a large pan, smooth the top with the hand dipped in cold water, let it stand a short time, and bake five or six hours in a Majestic Range. If put in the oven late in the day let it remain all night. Graham may be used instead of rye, and baked as above. In the olden time it was placed in kettle, allowed to rise, then placed on the hearth before the fire, with coals on top of lid, and baked.

Rye Bread.—Make a sponge of one quart warm water, one teacup yeast, thickened with rye flour; put in warm place to rise over night; scald one pint corn meal; when cool add it to sponge, and add rye flour till thick enough to knead, knead but little, let rise, mold into loaves, place in deep pie tins or small pudding-pans, let rise, and bake in a Majestic Range. Or, thicken the sponge with rye flour, and proceed as above. Wheat sponge may be used instead of rye.

The Best Ginger Bread.—One and one-half cups of molasses, one-half cup of brown sugar, one-half cup of butter, one-half cup of sweet milk, one teaspoonful of soda, one teaspoonful each extracts of cinnamon and ginger. Bake in shallow pan in a Majestic Range.

Buttered Toast.—Although toast is commonly used few know how to prepare it nicely. Take bread not too fresh, cut thin and evenly, trim off the crust edges for the crumb jar; first warm each side of the bread, then present the first side again to the fire until it takes on a rich, even, brown color; treat the other side in the same way; butter and serve immediately. The coals should be bright and hot. Toast properly made is very digestible, because all the moisture is extracted, and the bread has become pure farina of wheat; but when it is exposed to a hot fire and the outside charred, the inside remains as moist as ever, and butter applied to it while warm does not penetrate, but floats on the surface in the form of rancid oil. Or, beat one cup of butter and three tablespoons of flour to a cream, pour over this one and a half pints boiling water; place over a kettle of boiling water for ten minutes, dip into it the toast, and serve hot. Or, dip each slice of toast in boiling hot water (slightly salted), spread with butter, cover and keep hot.

Breakfast Toast.—Add to one-half pint of sweet milk two tablespoons sugar, a little salt and a well-beaten egg; dip in this slices of bread (if dry let it soak a minute), and fry on a buttered griddle on a Majestic Range until it is a light brown on each side. This is a good way to use dry bread.

Mennonite Toast.—Beat up three eggs well, add a pint of sweet milk and a pinch of salt; cut slices an inch thick from a loaf of baker's bread, remove crust, dip slices into the eggs and milk, fry like doughnuts in very hot lard or drippings till a delicate brown, on a Majestic Range, butter, and sprinkle with powdered sugar, and serve hot.

MAJESTIC RANGE No. 42.

FOR SOFT COAL OR WOOD.

IF FOR HARD COAL OR WOOD No. 42HC.

This range in dimensions is exactly the same as No. 40, the 15-gallon copper reservoir, as shown, making the change in the number. Descriptive words cannot do justice to this valuable kitchen utensil. To be appreciated it must be seen and used. Its adornments are simple, not too much, not too little, but just enough nickel-plate and polish to show to the best advantage.

Price, $53.00.

Prices include delivery on board cars in St. Louis. Freight must be paid by purchasers—the rate varying according to distance—from 25c to $2.00 per 100 lbs.

BISCUITS, ROLLS, TEA CAKES, ETC.

Biscuit.—Dissolve one rounded tablespoon of butter in a pint of hot milk; when lukewarm stir in one quart of flour, add one beaten egg, a little salt, and a teacup of yeast; work into dough until smooth. If winter, set in a warm place; if summer, in a cool one to rise. In the morning work softly and roll out one-half inch and cut into biscuit and set to rise for thirty minutes, when they will be ready to bake in a Majestic Range. These are delicious.

Soda Biscuit.—Put one quart of flour, before sifting, into sieve, with one teaspoon soda and two of cream tartar (or three of baking powder), one of salt, and one tablespoon white sugar; mix all thoroughly with the flour, run through sieve, rub in one level tablespoon of lard or butter (or half and half), wet with half pint sweet milk, roll on board about an inch thick, cut with biscuit cutter, and bake in a Majestic Range in a quick oven fifteen minutes. If you have not milk, use a little more butter, and wet with water. Handle as little and make as rapidly as possible.

Hard Tea Biscuit.—Two pounds of flour, one-fourth pound butter, one saltspoon salt, three gills milk; cut up the butter and rub it in the flour, add the salt and milk, knead dough for half an hour, cut cakes about as large as a small teacup and half an inch thick, prick with a fork, and bake in a Majestic Range in a moderate oven until they are a delicate brown.

South Carolina Biscuit.—One quart sweet cream or milk, one and a half cups butter or fresh lard, two tablespoons white sugar, one good teaspoon salt; add flour sufficient to make a stiff dough, knead well and mold into neat, small biscuit with the hands, as our grandmothers used to do; add one good teaspoon cream tartar if preferred; bake well in a Majestic Range, and you have good sweet biscuit that will keep for weeks in a dry place, and are very nice for traveling lunch. They are such as we used to send to the army, and the "boys" relished them "hugely."

Breakfast Rolls.—Mix the dough in the evening, according to directions in the recipe for making good bread; add a tablespoon of butter, and set where it will be a little warm until morning; cut off pieces, and carefully shape them into rolls of the desired size by rolling them between the hands, but do not knead them; dip the sides of each into drawn butter when they are shaped, and place them in the baking pan (the butter prevents their sticking together when baked, and they will be smooth and perfect when separated). Rub them over the top with drawn butter, and dust a little fine salt over the top; set in a warm place, and they will quickly rise ready for baking in a Majestic Range. These are delicious.

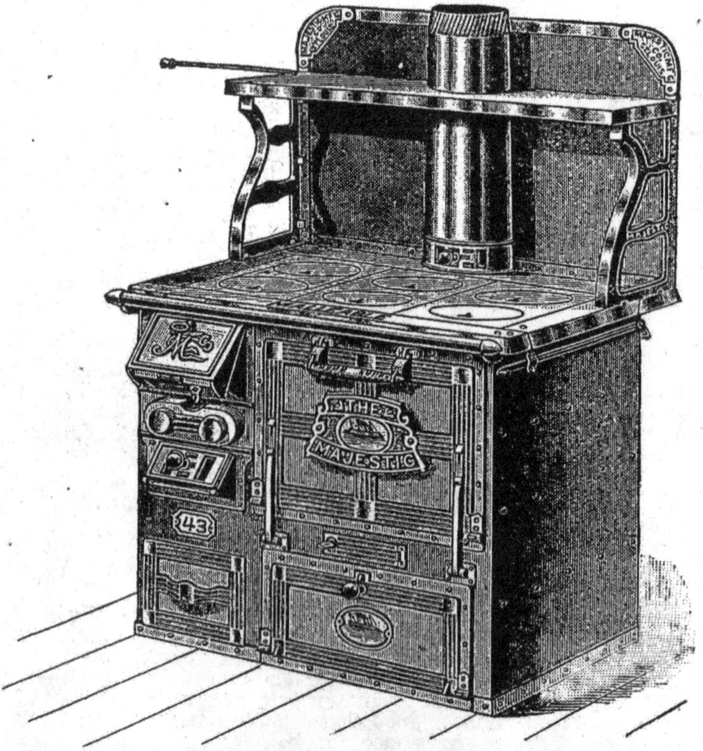

MAJESTIC RANGE No. 43.

FOR SOFT COAL OR WOOD.

IF FOR HARD COAL OR WOOD No. 43HC.

Has no water-front. Has three anchor plates and six 8-inch lids. Top cooking surface 29 x 33 inches; oven 17 inches wide, 21 inches deep, 13 inches high; mantel shelf, large lower warming oven, bailed ash pan, heavy diagonal grates and fire-linings, protecting bar, gravity door handle and towel rod. Flue lined with pure asbestos board. Made almost entirely of malleable iron and wrought steel. Progression is our motto, and the successive steps leading up to this beautiful range can be clearly observed.

Price, $44.00.

Prices include delivery on board cars in St. Louis. Freight must be paid by purchasers—the rate varying according to distance—from 25c to $2.00 per 100 lbs.

Coffee Rolls.—Work into a quart of bread dough a rounded tablespoon of butter and a half teacup of white sugar; add some dried currants (well washed and dried in the oven), sift some flour and sugar over them, work into the other ingredients, make into small rolls, dip into melted butter, place in tins, let rise a short time, and bake in a Majestic Range.

Every-day Rolls.—Take a piece of bread dough on baking day when molded out the last time, about enough for a small loaf, spread out a little, add one egg, two tablespoons of sugar, and three-fourths cup of lard; add a little flour and a small teaspoon soda if the least bit sour; mix well, let rise, mold into rolls or biscuits, set to rise again, and they will be ready for the oven in twenty or thirty minutes. Bake in a Majestic Range.

Vienna Rolls.—Have ready in a bowl a tablespoon of butter or lard, made soft by warming a little, and stirring with a spoon. Add to one quart of unsifted flour two heaping teaspoons baking powder; mix and sift thoroughly together, and place in a bowl with butter. Take more or less sweet milk as may be necessary to form a dough of usual stiffness, according to the flour (about three-fourths of a pint), put into the milk half a teaspoon of salt, and then stir it into the flour, etc., with a spoon, forming the dough, which turn out on a board and knead sufficiently to make smooth. Roll out half an inch thick and cut with a large round cutter; fold each one over to form a half round, wetting a little between the folds to make them stick together; place on buttered pans so as not to touch, wash over on top with milk to give them a gloss, and bake immediately in a hot oven in a Majestic Range about twenty minutes. It will do them no harm to stand half an hour before baking if it is desired.

Sally Lunn.—Sift into a pan a pound and a half of flour, put in two ounces of butter warmed in a pint of new milk, one saltspoon salt, three eggs well-beaten, and two tablespoons of good yeast. Mix well together, and put the whole into a tin pan well greased, and set to rise all night. Bake a little brown in a quick Majestic Range oven. Warm the milk and butter over water until the butter is melted; beat the eggs in a two-quart tin pail, and if the milk is not hot pour it over them. Stir in half the flour, then add the yeast, stirring thoroughly with the rest of the flour. Let rise over night. Some add two tablespoons sugar and use a teaspoon soda and two of cream tartar instead of the yeast.

Rusk.—One pint milk, three eggs, one teacup each of butter and sugar, and one coffee cup potato yeast; thicken with flour and sponge over night; in the morning stir down, let rise, and stir down again; when it rises make into a loaf, and let rise again; then roll out like soda biscuit, cut and put in pans, and, when light, bake carefully. Or, when baking take four cups dough, one-half cup butter, one cup sugar, three eggs; mix thoroughly, adding enough flour to mold easily; let rise, make into rather high and narrow biscuit, let rise again, rub the tops with a little sugar and water, then sprinkle over them dry sugar. Bake twenty minutes in a Majestic Range.

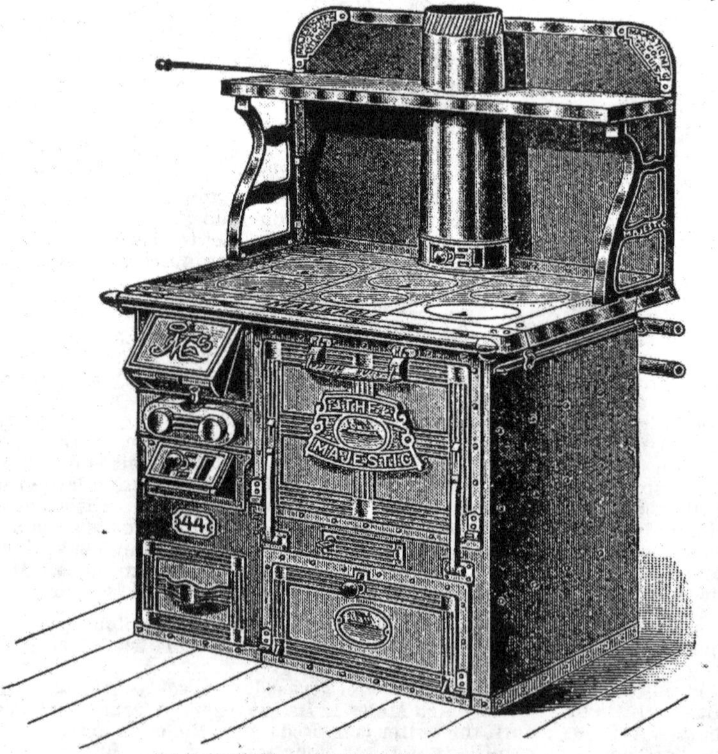

MAJESTIC RANGE No. 44.

FOR SOFT COAL OR WOOD.

IF FOR HARD COAL OR WOOD No. 44HC.

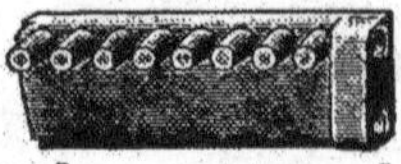

The only pronounced change from No. 43, is that this range has our "pin extension" water-front; and the all-important question with housekeepers, what range will supply the greatest quantity of hot water is at once answered when this heater is shown in the range. There is nothing made, encompassed in the same space, that is equal to it in heating power.

Price, $46.00.

Prices include delivery on board cars in St. Louis. Freight must be paid by purchasers—the rate varying according to distance—from 25c to $2.00 per 100 lbs.

Rusk.—Two teacups raised dough, one teacup sugar, half cup butter, two well-beaten eggs, flour enough to make a stiff dough; set to rise, and when light mold into high biscuit and let rise again; sift sugar and cinnamon over the top and place in Majestic Range oven.

Lebanon Rusk.—One cup mashed potatoes, one of sugar, one of home-made yeast, three eggs; mix together; when raised light, add half cup butter or lard, and flour to make a soft dough, and, when quite light, mold into small cakes, and let them rise again before baking in a Majestic Range. If wanted for tea, set about nine A. M.

Bread Puffs.—If the wheat bread is light enough for the oven at breakfast time, have ready some hot lard in a deep kettle; with the thumb and two fingers pull up some of the dough quite thin, and cut it some two or three inches in length; as these pieces are cut, drop them in the lard and fry like doughnuts on a Majestic Range. At table they are eaten like biscuit; they may also be served in a vegetable dish with a dressing of hot cream, seasoned with pepper and salt.

Wheaten Gems.—Mix one teaspoon baking powder and a little salt into one pint flour; add to the beaten yolks of two eggs one teacup sweet milk or cream, a piece of butter (melted) half the size of an egg, the flour with baking powder and salt mixed, and the well-beaten whites of the two eggs. Beat well, bake immediately in gem pans in a hot Majestic Range oven, and take out and send to the table immediately.

Wheat Muffins.—Mix one pint milk, two eggs, three tablespoons yeast, and saltspoon of salt, with flour enough to make a stiff batter; let rise four or five hours and bake in muffin rings in hot Majestic Range oven for about ten minutes. This recipe may be made with Graham flour by adding two tablespoons of molasses, and is excellent.

Corn Muffins.—One quart sifted Indian meal, a heaping teaspoon butter, one quart milk, a saltspoon salt, a third cup yeast, a tablespoon of molasses; let it rise four or five hours, and bake in muffin-rings in a Majestic Range.

Graham Muffins.—Two cups of sour milk, two tablespoons brown sugar, a little salt, one teaspoon soda, sufficient Graham flour to make moderately stiff. If not convenient to use sour milk use sweet, adding cream of tartar. Bake in a Majestic Range.

Waffles.—Take one quart of flour, a teaspoon of salt, a tablespoon of melted butter, and milk enough to make a thick batter. Mix thoroughly. Add two well-beaten eggs, and one measure each of acid and soda (or two heaping teaspoons acid and one moderately heaping teaspoon soda) of Horsford's Bread Preparation; stir well, and bake at once in waffle irons on a Majestic Range.

Quick Waffles.—Two pints sweet milk, one cup butter (melted), sifted flour to make a soft batter; add the well-beaten yolks of six eggs, then the beaten whites, and lastly (just before baking) four teaspoons baking powder, beating very hard and fast for a few minutes. These are very good with four or five eggs, but much better with more. Bake in a Majestic Range.

Crullers.—Two coffee cups sugar, one of sweet milk, three eggs, a heaping tablespoon butter, three teaspoons baking powder mixed with six cups flour, half a nutmeg and a level teaspoon cinnamon. Beat eggs, sugar and butter together, add milk, spices and flour; put another cup flour on molding board, turn the dough out on it, and knead until stiff enough to roll out to a quarter inch thick; cut in squares, make three or four incisions in each square, lift by taking alternate strips between the finger and thumb, drop into hot lard and cook like doughnuts on a Majestic Range.

Fried Cakes.—One coffee cup of not too thick sour cream, or one of sour milk and one tablespoon of butter, two eggs, a little nutmeg and salt, one teacup sugar, one small teaspoon soda dissolved; mix soft. Fry on a Majestic Range.

Cornmeal Doughnuts.—A teacup and a half boiling milk poured over two teacups meal; when cool add two cups flour, one of butter, one and one-half of sugar, three eggs; flavor with nutmeg or cinnamon; let rise till very light; roll about half an inch thick, cut in diamond shape and boil in hot lard on a Majestic Range.

Cream Doughnuts.—Beat one cup of sour cream and sugar and two eggs together, add level teaspoon soda, a little salt, and flour enough to roll. Cook on a Majestic Range.

Doughnuts.—One egg, a cup rich milk, a cup sugar, three pints flour, three teaspoons baking powder (or one and a half measures Horsford's Bread Preparation). These are made richer by adding one egg and one teaspoon butter. Cook on a Majestic Range.

North Star Doughnuts.—One and a half cups sugar, one of sour milk, half cup butter, three eggs, a level teaspoon soda, spice to taste, and flour to roll. Cook on a Majestic Range.

Berlin Pancakes.—Roll out dough slightly sweetened and shortened, as if for very plain doughnuts; cut in circles like biscuit, put a teaspoon currant jam or jelly on the center of one, lay another upon it, press the edges tightly together with the fingers and fry quickly in boiling fat on a Majestic Range. They will be perfect globes when done, a little smaller than an orange.

Trifles.—A quart flour, a cup sugar, two tablespoons melted butter, a little salt, two teaspoons baking powder, one egg, and sweet milk sufficient to make rather stiff; roll out in thin sheets, cut in pieces about two by four inches; make as many cuts across the short way as possible, inserting the knife near one edge and ending the cut just before reaching the other. Pass two knitting needles under every other strip, spread the needles as far apart as possible, and with them hold the trifles in the fat until a light brown. Only one can be fried at a time. Fry on a Majestic Range.

Lemon Snaps.—A large cup sugar, two-thirds cup butter, half teaspoon soda dissolved in two teaspoons hot water, flour enough to roll thin; flavor with lemon. Bake in a Majestic Range.

Fruit Cookies.—Two cups of sugar, one cup of butter, two cups of chopped raisins, two eggs, two tablespoonfuls of sour milk, one teaspoonful of soda, one-half teaspoonful each of extract of nutmeg, clove and cinnamon. Flour enough to roll; bake in a quick Majestic Range oven.

The Best Cookies.—Two cups of powdered sugar, one-half cup of butter, one cup of sweet milk, whites of four eggs, one teaspoonful extract of lemon, two teaspoonfuls of baking powder, flour enough to make a soft batter. Bake in patty tins in a Majestic Range. Beat the batter hard for ten minutes before putting into tins. When cold, ice with soft white icing made with the whites of four eggs and powdered sugar enough to make them stiff.

Tea Cakes.—Put upon a pie board one pound of flour which you have previously sifted, make a hole in the center, in which place one-half pound of butter, six ounces of powdered sugar and four eggs. Mix all well together, and roll out your paste extremely thin; cut it out in rounds or squares, put in a pan which has been buttered slightly, brush your cakes with beaten egg, sprinkle on top with one-half pound of currants; put in a Majestic Range oven, and when colored a bright yellow remove them and serve as needed.

Almond Drops.—Six eggs, one pound of sugar, one-half pound of butter, one quart of flour, two teaspoonfuls of baking powder, one cup of cream, one teaspoonful extract of almond. Drop from spoon on buttered paper, and bake in a Majestic Range.

Anise Drops.—Three cups of sugar and six eggs beaten together one-half hour; add one quart of flour, one teaspoonful of anise seed. Grease the pan with beeswax, and drop the mixture from a spoon. Bake in a Majestic Range.

Spice Drops.—Yolks of three eggs, one-half cup of butter, one cup of molasses, one-half cup of sweet milk, three cups of flour, three teaspoonfuls of baking powder; spice with ground nutmeg, cloves, cinnamon, and flavor with one teaspoonful extract of lemon; drop on tins lined with buttered paper. Bake quickly in Majestic Range.

Dew Drops.—Two cups of powdered sugar, one-half cup of butter, one cup of sweet milk, whites of four eggs, one teaspoonful extract of lemon, two teaspoonfuls of baking powder, flour enough to make a soft batter. Bake in patty tins in Majestic Range, and ice when cold.

Ginger Drops.—One cup of molasses, one-half cup of brown sugar, one-half cup of butter, one teaspoonful each extract of ginger and cinnamon; two teaspoonfuls of soda in one cup of hot water, three cups of flour, two eggs. Bake in drops in buttered tins in Majestic Range.

Bread Cake.—On baking day, take from your dough when ready for baking, two cups of dough, add two cups of white sugar, one cup of butter, three eggs, two tablespoonfuls of sweet cream; one-half pound of currants, dredged; one and one-half teaspoonfuls extract of cinnamon; beat hard for five minutes; put in two buttered pans and let raise for twenty minutes. Bake one-half hour in a Majestic Range.

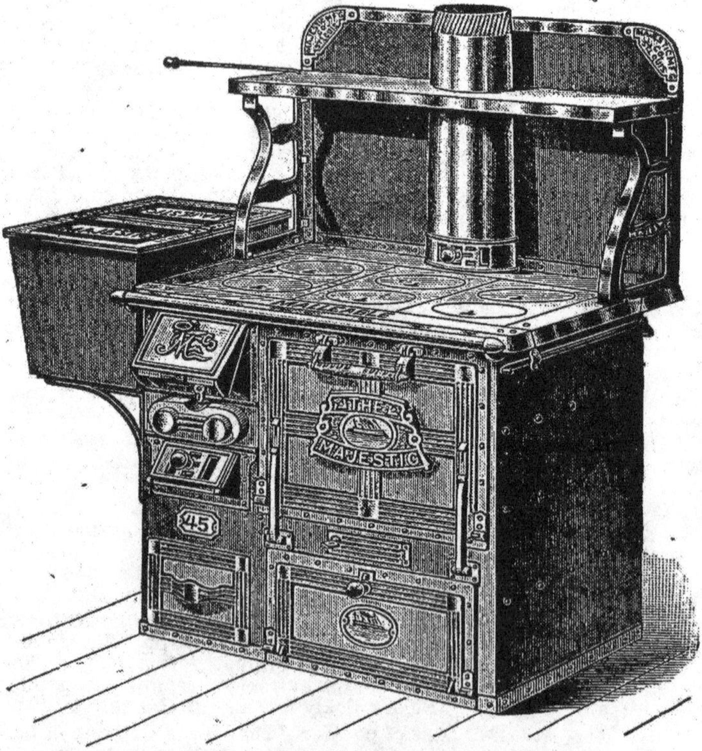

MAJESTIC RANGE No. 45.

FOR SOFT COAL OR WOOD.

IF FOR HARD COAL OR WOOD No. 45HC.

Long descriptive articles are tiresome, hence we refer for detail to No. 43, the only distinguishing feature in this range being the 15-gallon copper reservoir and its connections, as shown. It is needless to say that all users are delighted.

Price, $54.00.

Prices include delivery on board cars in St. Louis. Frieght must be paid by purchasers—the rate varying according to distance—from 25c to $2.00 per 100 lbs.

Rice Waffles.—Boil half a pint of rice and let it get cold, mix with it one-fourth pound butter and a little salt. Sift in it one and a half pints flour, beat five eggs separately, stir the yolks together with one quart milk, add whites beaten to a stiff froth, beat hard, and bake at once in waffle-iron on Majestic Range.

Corn Dodgers.—To one quart corn meal add a little salt and a small tablespoon lard; scald with boiling water and beat hard for a few minutes; drop a large spoonful in a well-greased pan. The batter should be thick enough to just flatten on the bottom, leaving them quite high in the center. Bake in a hot Majestic Range oven.

Cracknells.—To one pint of rich milk put two ounces butter and spoon of yeast. Make it warm, and mix enough fine flour to make a light dough; roll thin and cut in long pieces, two inches broad. Prick well, and bake in a slow oven in Majestic Range.

Alabama Johnny-Cake.—Cook a pint of rice till tender on a Majestic Range, add a tablespoon butter; when cold add two beaten eggs and one pint of meal, and when mixed spread on an oaken board and bake by tipping the board up before an open fire. When done on one side turn over. The dough should be spread half an inch thick.

Johnny-Cake.—Two-thirds teaspoon soda, three tablespoons sugar, one teaspoon cream of tartar, one egg, one cup sweet milk, six tablespoons Indian meal, three tablespoons flour and a little salt. This makes a thin batter. Bake in a Majestic Range.

Alabama Rice Fritters.—Four eggs beaten very light, one pint milk, one cup boiled rice, three teaspoons baking powder in one quart flour; make into a batter, drop by spoonfuls into boiling lard. Cook on a Majestic Range.

Sauce.—One pound of sugar, one and a half cups water, stick of cinnamon; boil until clear.

Apple Fritters.—Make a batter in proportion of one cup sweet milk to two cups flour, a heaping teaspoon baking powder, two eggs beaten separately, one tablespoon sugar, one saltspoon salt; heat the milk a little more than milk-warm, add slowly to the beaten yolks and sugar, then add flour and whites of eggs; stir all together and throw in thin slices of good sour apples, dipping the batter up over them; drop in boiling lard in large spoonfuls with piece of apple in each and fry to a light brown on a Majestic Range. Serve with maple syrup or a nice syrup made of sugar.

Cream Fritters.—One and a half pints flour, one pint milk, six well-beaten eggs, one-half nutmeg, two teaspoons salt, one pint cream; stir the whole enough to mix the cream; fry in small cakes on a Majestic Range.

Fritters.—Four eggs well beaten, one quart of flour, two heaping teaspoonfuls baking powder, one-half teaspoonful of salt, milk to make a batter; fry in hot lard on a Majestic Range; sprinkle with sugar, or eat with syrup.

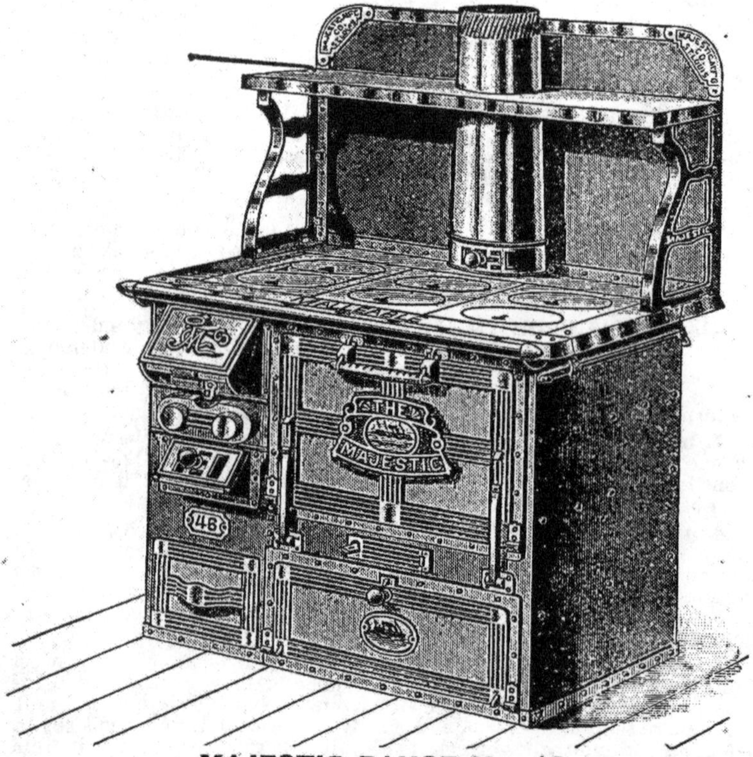

MAJESTIC RANGE No. 46.

FOR SOFT COAL OR WOOD.

IF FOR HARD COAL OR WOOD No. 46HC.

Has no water-front. It is the realization of all that is good and honest in a cooking apparatus. Is perfect in construction, operates charmingly, and will do service for from twelve to fifteen persons. Top cooking surface 29x36 inches; six 8-inch lids; oven 20 inches wide, 21 inches deep, 13 inches high; mantel shelf, large lower warming oven, bailed ash pan, heavy diagonal grates and fire-linings, protecting bar, gravity door handle and towel rod. Flue lined with pure asbestos board. Made almost entirely of malleable iron and wrought steel.

Price, $48.00.

Prices include delivery on board cars in St. Louis. Freight must be paid by purchasers—the rate varying according to distance—from 25c to $2.00 per 100 lbs.

Buckwheat Cakes.—Buckwheat flour when properly ground is perfectly free from grits. The grain should be run through the smutter with a strong blast before grinding, and the greatest care taken through the whole process. Adulteration with rye or corn cheapens the flour but injures the quality. The pure buckwheat is best and is unsurpassed for griddle-cakes. To make batter, warm one pint sweet milk and one pint water (one may be cold and the other boiling); put half the mixture in a stone crock, add five teacups buckwheat flour, beat well until smooth, add the rest of the milk and water, and last a teacup of yeast. Or, the same ingredients and proportions may be used except adding two tablespoons of molasses or sugar, and using one quart of water instead of one pint each of milk and water. Cook on a Majestic Range.

French Pancakes.—Beat together till smooth six eggs and half a pound of flour, melt four ounces butter and add to the batter with one ounce of sugar and half a pint of milk, and beat until smooth. Put a tablespoon at a time into a hot frying-pan slightly greased, spreading the batter evenly over the surface of the pan by tipping it about, fry to a light brown on a Majestic Range, spread with jelly, roll it up, dust it with powdered sugar, and serve hot.

Bread Cakes.—Take stale bread and soak over night in sour milk; in the morning rub through a colander, and to one quart add the yolks of two eggs, one teaspoon salt, one teaspoon soda, two tablespoons sugar, and flour enough to make batter little thicker than for buckwheat cakes; add last the well-beaten whites of the eggs and bake on a Majestic Range.

Corn Cakes.—One pint cornmeal, one of sour milk or buttermilk, one egg, one teaspoon soda, one of salt. A tablespoon of flour or corn starch may be used in place of eggs. Bake on a griddle on a Majestic Range.

Flannel Cakes.—Make hot a pint of sweet milk and into it put two heaping tablespoons butter, let melt, then add a pint of cold milk, the well-beaten yolks of four eggs—placing the whites in a cold place—a teaspoon of salt, four tablespoons potato yeast, and sufficient flour to make a stiff batter; set in a warm place to rise, let stand three hours or over night; before baking add the beaten whites; fry like any other griddle-cakes on a Majestic Range. Be sure to make batter stiff enough, for flour must not be added in the morning unless it is allowed to rise again.

Indian Pancakes.—One pint Indian meal, one teaspoon salt, small teaspoon soda; pour on boiling water until a little thinner than mush; let stand until cool, add the yolks of four eggs, half a cup of flour in which is mixed two teaspoons cream tartar; stir in as much sweet milk or water as will make the batter suitable to bake; beat the whites well and add just before baking in a Majestic Range.

Plantation Buckwheat Cakes.—One quart best buckwheat flour, one handful of corn meal, two teaspoonfuls baking powder, one teaspoonful salt, two tablespoonfuls New Orleans molasses, one tablespoonful melted butter. Mix thoroughly; cook on a Majestic Range, as soon as ready.

MAJESTIC RANGE No. 47.

FOR SOFT COAL OR WOOD.

IF FOR HARD COAL OR WOOD No. 47HC.

With our "pin extension" water-front connected with 40 or 50 gallon pressure boiler, this range furnishes the most abundant supply of hot water, and it is not too much to say, that it charms the cook and supplies at each meal time the utmost wants of the household. It is recommended as possessing all the requisites to economical housekeeping.

Price, $50.00.

Prices include delivery on board cars in St. Louis. Freight must be paid by purchasers—the rate varying according to distance—from 25c to $2.00 per 100 lbs.

Fried Mush.—A delicious breakfast relish is made by slicing cold mush thin and frying in a little hot lard on a Majestic Range. Or dip in beaten eggs salted to taste, then in bread or cracker crumbs, and drop in hot lard like doughnuts.

Graham Mush.—Sift meal slowly into boiling salted water, stirring briskly until it is as thick as can be stirred with one hand; serve with milk or cream and sugar, or butter and syrup. It is much improved by removing from the kettle to a pan as soon as thoroughly mixed, and steaming for three or four hours. It may also be eaten cold, or sliced and fried like corn mush. Cook on a Majestic Range.

Oatmeal Mush.—To two quarts boiling water well salted add one and a half cups best oatmeal (Irish, Scotch, Canadian or Akron are best); stir in meal by degrees, and after stirring up a few times to prevent its settling down in a mass at the bottom, leave it to cook three hours without stirring. While stirring in the meal put inner kettle directly on range. (Cook in a custard kettle with water in outer kettle). To cook for breakfast it may be put on over night, allowing it to boil an hour or two in the evening, but it is better when freshly cooked. Serve with cream and sugar. This is unsurpassed as a breakfast dish, especially for growing children, who need bone and muscle-producing food. To be wholesome it must be well cooked, and not the pasty, half-cooked mass usually served at boarding-houses. There are a few persons with very delicate digestive powers who should eat oatmeal only when thoroughly pearled, as the outer husks of the grain irritate the coatings of the stomach. In lieu of a custard kettle the mush may be made in a pan or small tin bucket, and then placed in a steamer and steamed two hours on a Majestic Range.

Steamed Oatmeal.—To one teacup oatmeal add one quart cold water, teaspoon salt; put in steamer over a kettle of cold water, and steam one hour and a half on a Majestic Range after meal begins to cook.

Cracked Wheat.—Two quarts salted water to two cups best white winter wheat; boil two or three hours in a custard kettle. Or, soak over night and boil at least three-fourths of an hour. Or, put boiling water in a pan or small tin bucket, set on range, stir in wheat, set in steamer and steam four hours. Or, make a strong sack of thick muslin or drilling, moisten wheat with cold water, add a little salt, place in sack, leaving half the space for wheat to swell in. Fit a round sheet of tin, perforated with holes half an inch in diameter, to the inside of ordinary kettle so that it will rest two or three inches from the bottom; lay sack on the tin, put in water enough to reach tin, and boil from three to four hours, supplying water as it evaporates. Serve with butter and syrup, or cream and sugar. When cold, slice and fry on a Majestic Range; or warm with a little milk and salt in a pan greased with a little butter; or make in griddle-cakes with a batter of eggs, milk, a little flour and pinch of salt.

Fine White Hominy or Grits.—Take two cups to two quarts salted water, soak over night, and boil three-quarters of an hour in a custard kettle on a Majestic Range. Serve with milk and sugar, or when cold slice and fry.

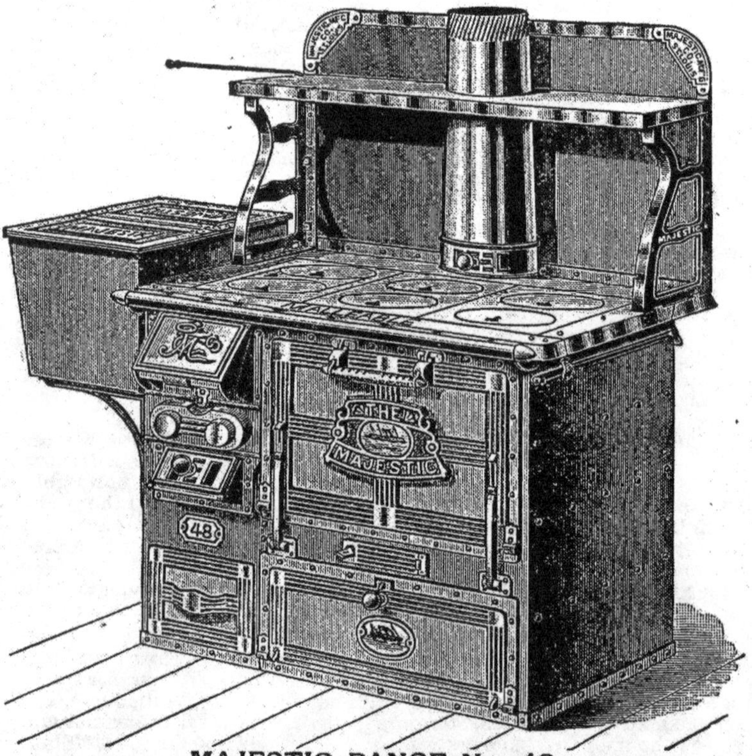

MAJESTIC RANGE No. 48.

FOR SOFT COAL OR WOOD.

IF FOR HARD COAL OR WOOD No. 48HC.

In all things pertaining to culinary matters this range stands preeminent. With its improvements the services of the cook can be nearly dispensed with; it does its work noiselessly, and with great comfort to the user. With its 15-gallon copper reservoir attachments the hot water supply is abundant. In other respects it is the same as No. 46.

Price, $60.00.

Prices include delivery on board cars in St. Louis. Freight must be paid by purchasers—the rate varying according to distance—from 25c to $2.00 per 100 lbs.

CAKES.

Cup Cake.—One cup of butter, two cups of sugar, three cups of flour, four eggs, one-half cup of milk, two teaspoonfuls of baking powder, one teaspoonful extract of lemon or white rose. Bake in a Majestic Range.

Plain Fruit Cake.—One cup of butter, one of brown sugar, one of molasses, one of sweet milk, three cups of flour, four eggs, one and one-half teaspoonfuls of cream of tartar, one teaspoonful of soda, one of nutmeg, two pounds of raisins, seeded; one teaspoonful each extract of rose and cinnamon, one-half of cloves, one-half wineglass of brandy. Bake in a Majestic Range.

Cream Sponge Cake.—Two cups of sugar, one of cream, two cups of flour, four eggs, one teaspoonful of baking powder, one teaspoonful extract of lemon. Bake quickly in a Majestic Range.

Pound Sponge Cake.—One pound of sugar, one-half pound of flour, nine eggs, juice of one lemon; stir the yolks of eggs and sugar to a cream; add flour and lemon; the whites last, and bake in a quick oven in a Majestic Range.

Quick Sponge Cake.—Three eggs, one and one-half cups of sugar, two cups of flour, two teaspoonfuls of baking powder, one-half cup of cold water, one teaspoonful extract of lemon. Bake in a Majestic Range.

White Sponge Cake.—One and one-half cups of powdered sugar, one cup of flour, a pinch of salt, whites of eleven eggs, one teaspoonful of baking powder, one teaspoonful extract of vanilla. Bake in a Majestic Range.

Marble Cake.—*White Part.*—One-half cup of butter, one and one-half cups of sugar, one-half cup of milk, two and one-half cups of flour, whites of four eggs, one teaspoonful of baking powder, one teaspoonful extract of lemon.

Dark Part.—One-half cup of butter, one-half cup of molasses, two cups of brown sugar, one-half cup of sour milk, one-half teaspoonful of soda, two cups of flour, yolks of four eggs, one whole egg, one teaspoonful of cloves, one of extract of cinnamon; put into well-buttered pan, one teaspoonful of white, one of dark, until all is used. Bake in a Majestic Range.

Chocolate Marble Cake.—Whites of six eggs, one cup of butter, two cups of sugar, three cups of flour, one-half cup of sweet milk, two teaspoonfuls of baking powder, one teaspoonful extract of vanilla; one-quarter cake of chocolate grated and mixed into one-half of the batter; put into the cake pan in layers of dark, then white. Bake in a Majestic Range.

MAJESTIC RANGE No. 49.

FOR SOFT COAL OR WOOD.

IF FOR HARD COAL OR WOOD No. 49HC.

Has no water-front. This range is made more particularly for the North and Northwestern trade, where people want 9-inch lids and large ovens. Top cooking surface 31x33 inches; four 9-inch lids and wide key-plate; oven 17 inches wide, 23 inches deep, 13 inches high; mantel shelf, large lower warming oven, bailed ash pan, heavy diagonal grates and fire-linings, protecting bar, gravity door handle and towel rod. Flue lined with pure asbestos board. The general design and construction is the same as on all family sizes. Price, $45.00.

Prices include delivery on board cars in St. Louis. Freight must be paid by purchasers—the rate varying according to distance—from 25c to $2.00 per 100 lbs.

Bride's Cake.—Three cups of white sugar, one cup of butter, one of sweet milk, four cups of flour, one-half cup of corn starch, whites of twelve eggs, two teaspoonfuls of baking powder, one teaspoonful each of extract of vanilla and lemon. Bake in a Majestic Range.

Black or Wedding Cake.—One pound of brown sugar, one pound of butter, one and one-half pounds of flour, twelve eggs; one pound of currants, dredged; two pounds of raisins, seeded; one-half pound of citron, cut thin; one-half pound figs, chopped; one pound almonds, blanched and chopped; one glass of jelly, one wineglass of brandy, one teaspoonful extract of cinnamon, one teaspoonful of cloves, two teaspoonfuls of nutmeg.

Mix all well, the whites of the eggs and brandy last. Bake in two loaves in a Majestic Range four hours, or longer if not cooked through. Will keep well for one year.

Angels' Food No. 1.—One and one-half tumblers of granulated sugar, one tumbler flour, each sifted seven times; in the last sifting put in one even teaspoonful of cream of tartar; whites of eleven eggs; flavor with extract of almond or vanilla. Bake one hour in a Majestic Range.

Angels' Food No. 2.—One and one-half tumblers of sifted powdered sugar, one tumbler of flour sifted four times, one teaspoonful of baking powder, whites of eleven eggs, one teaspoonful extract of vanilla; beat the eggs stiff, add sugar, then flour and baking powder. Do not butter the pan. Bake one hour in a Majestic Range.

Fig Cake.—Two cups of sugar, one cup of butter, one cup of cold water, three cups of seeded raisins, one pound of figs, three cups of flour, two teaspoonfuls of baking powder, one egg. Bake slowly in a Majestic Range.

Imperial Cake.—One pound of butter, one pound of sugar, one pound of flour, juice and rind of one lemon, nine eggs, one pound of blanched almonds, one-half pound of citron, one-half pound of raisins, one teaspoonful of baking powder. Bake in a Majestic Range.

Fruit Cake.—Stir to a cream one pound each of brown sugar and butter and ten eggs; one wineglass of brandy, one of wine; mix in one pound of flour and two teaspoonfuls of baking powder; add two pounds of seeded raisins, two of currants, one of citron, one-quarter of almonds. One teaspoonful each extract of rose and cinnamon. Bake in a Majestic Range three or four hours.

Washington Cake.—One cup of butter, three cups of brown sugar, one cup of milk, four eggs, one cup of seeded raisins, three cups of flour, two teaspoonfuls of baking powder, one teaspoonful of cloves, one of nutmeg, one teaspoonful extract of cinnamon. Bake in a Majestic Range.

Hickory-Nut Cake.—Two cups of sugar, one cup butter, three cups of flour, one cup of milk, four eggs, two teaspoonfuls of baking powder, one cup of nut meats cut fine, one-half teaspoonful extract of almond. Bake in a Mejestic Range.

MAJESTIC RANGE No. 50.

FOR SOFT COAL OR WOOD.

IF FOR HARD COAL OR WOOD No. 50HC.

Is a fac-simile of No. 49. The only change, to which we call attention, is for the guidance of people in ordering. This range has our "pin extension" water-front fitted with nipples ready for connection with pressure boiler, and if properly connected, insures a supply of hot water beyond the needs of any one family.

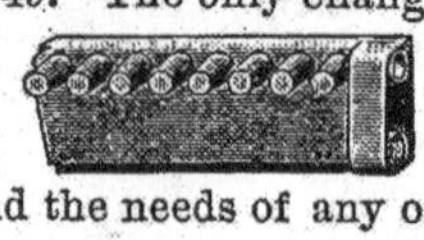

Price, $47.00.

Prices include delivery on board cars in St. Louis. Freight must be paid by purchasers—the rate varying according to distance—from 25c to $2.00 per 100 lbs.

Chocolate Loaf Cake.—One cup of sugar, one tablespoonful of melted butter, three-fourths cup of milk, one and one-half cups of flour, two teaspoonfuls of baking powder, yolks of eight eggs, white of one; grate one-quarter of a cake of chocolate into one-half cup of the milk and boil until thick. Flavor with extract of vanilla and mix into the batter. Bake in a Majestic Range.

Cocoanut Loaf Cake.—One pint of flour, two cups of sugar, one-half cup of butter, one cup of milk, five eggs, two teaspoonfuls of baking powder, one cup of grated cocoanut, one-half teaspoonful extract of almond. Bake in a Majestic Range.

Caramel Cake.—One cup of butter, two cups of sugar, one cup of milk, one and one-half cups of flour, one cup of corn starch, whites of seven eggs, two teaspoonfuls of baking powder, one teaspoonful extract of vanilla; bake in long pans. One-half pound of brown sugar, one-half pound of chocolate, one-half cup of milk, butter the size of an egg, two teaspoonfuls extract of vanilla; boil until thick enough to spread; spread over the top and sides of cake. Or two cups of brown sugar, one cup of sweet cream, two teaspoonfuls of vanilla, butter the size of an egg; boil until it sugars; spread over top and sides. Bake in a Majestic Range.

White Cream Cake.—Four cups of flour, one cup of butter, one cup of sweet cream, three cups of sugar, two teaspoonfuls of baking powder, whites of ten eggs; flavor with extract of white rose. Bake in a Majestic Range.

White Pound Cake.—One pound of sugar, one pound of flour, one pound of butter, whites of sixteen eggs, one teaspoonful of baking powder, one teaspoonful extract of lemon. Bake in a Majestic Range.

White Lady Cake.—One and one-half cups of flour, one cup of sugar, one-half cup of butter, whites of four eggs, one-half cup of milk, one teaspoonful of baking powder; flavor with extract of peach. Bake in a Majestic Range.

White Mountain Cake.—One pound of sugar, one and one-half pounds of butter, one pound of flour, whites of ten eggs, one-half teaspoonful extract of almond. Bake in a Majestic Range.

White Fruit Cake.—One pound each of flour, butter, white sugar and blanched almonds, two pounds of citron, one grated cocoanut, whites of sixteen eggs, two teaspoonfuls of baking powder, one teaspoonful extract of white rose. Bake in a Majestic Range.

Pound Cake No. 1.—One pound of butter, one pound of sugar, one pound of flour, sixteen eggs—leaving out yolks of four—one teaspoonful extract of lemon. Bake in a Majestic Range.

Pound Cake No. 2.—One pound of sugar, one pound of butter, one pound of flour, twelve eggs beaten separately very light, one wineglass of brandy. Bake in a Majestic Range.

Citron Cake.—One quart of flour, one cup of butter, two cups of sugar, twelve eggs, one cup of cream, one glass of wine, one teaspoonful extract of almond, one cup of chopped citron. Bake in a Majestic Range.

MAJESTIC RANGE No. 51.

FOR SOFT COAL OR WOOD.

IF FOR HARD COAL OR WOOD No. 51HC.

Has our 15-gallon copper reservoir, the recommending feature of which is the absence of nipples and closed water-back; such connections giving trouble to users on account of filling with sediment and burning out, or freezing and bursting. With our new connection this trouble cannot occur; the heater being open to the reservoir is safe and readily cleanable. For dimensions, see No. 49.

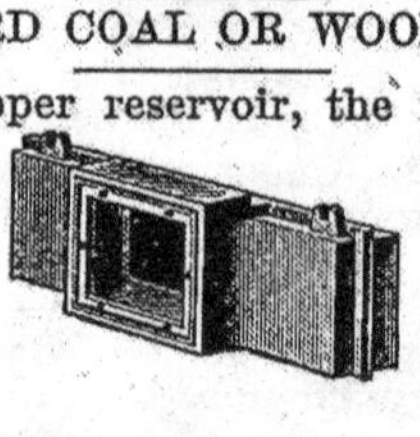

Price, $55.00.

Prices include delivery on board cars in St. Louis. Freight must be paid by purchasers—the rate varying according to distance—from 25c to $2.00 per 100 lbs.

Doughnuts.—One pound of butter, one and three-quarters of a pound of sugar, one quart of sweet milk, four eggs, one cup of yeast, one teaspoonful extract of cinnamon. Mix together butter, sugar, milk, yeast and one quart of flour. Set to raise over night. In the morning add the eggs well-beaten, then the flavoring, and flour enough to make a stiff dough; let rise three hours; roll thick and fry on a Majestic Range in hot lard.

Fried Cakes No. 1.—Take three eggs, one cup of brown sugar, one cup of sweet milk, three teaspoonfuls of baking powder, three tablespoonfuls of hot lard, one quart of flour, one teaspoonful of extract of cinnamon. Fry in hot lard on a Majestic Range.

Fried Cakes No. 2.—One quart of flour, one cup of sugar, one-half cup of milk, one-half cup of cream, two eggs, two teaspoonfuls of baking powder, one teaspoonful extract of cinnamon. Fry in hot lard on a Majestic Range.

Ginger Snaps. -One and one-quarter cups of flour, one-quarter cup of sugar, two tablespoonfuls of butter, one-half pint of molasses, three tablespoonfuls of baking powder, two teaspoonfuls extract of Jamaica ginger. Bake in a Majestic Range.

Ginger Cookies.—Two cups of molasses, one cup of lard, one cup of sugar, one-half cup of sour cream, one tablespoonful of ground ginger, two eggs, three and one-half teaspoonfuls of soda, flour to roll thick. Bake in quick Majestic Range oven.

Fruit Ginger Bread.—Two pounds of flour, three-fourths of a pound of butter, one pound of sugar; one pound of raisins, seeded and chopped; one pound of currants, two cups of molasses, one-half cup of sour cream, six eggs, one heaping teaspoonful of soda, two tablespoonfuls of ground ginger, one teaspoonful extract of cinnamon; mix well. Add the fruit last, well dredged with flour. Beat well, and bake in tin pans in a Majestic Range.

Ginger Bread.—One cup of molasses, one-half cup of butter, one cup of boiling water, one egg, two and one-half cups of flour, one and one-half teaspoonfuls of soda, one teaspoonful each essence of Jamaica ginger and extract of cinnamon. Bake in a Majestic Range.

Soft Sugar Ginger Bread.—One cup of molasses and two cups of sugar beaten together, one cup of sour milk, one teaspoonful of soda, four eggs, five cups of flour, and one and one-half tablespoonfuls of ground ginger. Bake thirty minutes in a Majestic Range.

Sponge Ginger Bread (Eggless).—Five cups of flour, one heaping tablespoonful of butter, one cup of molasses, one cup of sugar, one cup of sour milk, two teaspoonfuls of saleratus dissolved in hot water, two teaspoonfuls extract of ginger, one teaspoonful extract of cinnamon; beat very light, and bake in broad, shallow pans in a Majestic Range. Half a pound of seeded raisins, cut fine, added to this will make a delicious tea bread.

MAJESTIC RANGE No. 52.

FOR SOFT COAL OR WOOD.

IF FOR HARD COAL OR WOOD No. 52HC.

Has no water-front. Top cooking surface 31 x 36 inches; six 9-inch lids; oven 20 inches wide, 23 inches deep, 13 inches high; mantel shelf, large lower warming oven, bailed ash pan, heavy diagonal grates and fire-linings, protecting bar, gravity door handle and towel rod. Flue lined with pure asbestos board. Made almost entirely of malleable iron and wrought steel. This range is amply large to do the cooking for families of fifteen to twenty persons.

Price, $54.00.

Prices include delivery on board cars in St. Louis. Freight must be paid by purchasers—the rate varying according to distance—from 25c to $2.00 per 100 lbs.

Coffee Cake.—One cup of coffee or two tablespoonfuls extract of coffee, one cup of molasses, one cup of butter, one cup sugar, one of raisins, one of currants, four cups of flour, one nutmeg, one-half teaspoonful extract of cinnamon, one-half teaspoonful cloves, four eggs, one-half teaspoonful soda dissolved in hot water. Bake in a Majestic Range.

Clove Cake.—One cup brown sugar, one egg, one cup of sour cream, one teaspoonful of soda, one-half cup of flour, a pinch of salt, one teaspoonful of cloves. Bake in a Majestic Range.

Spice Cake.—One cup brown sugar, one cup molasses, one cup butter, one of milk, one nutmeg, one teaspoonful extract of cinnamon, one teaspoonful of cloves, three eggs, four cups of flour, two teaspoonfuls of baking powder. Bake in a Majestic Range.

Mottled Cake.—One pound of sugar, one-half pound of butter, whites of twelve eggs, three cups of flour, one teaspoonful of baking powder, one teaspoonful extract of peach; take one-half of the batter and stir in one teaspoonful fruit coloring; fill the buttered cake pan by putting in one spoonful of white, then one of pink, until all the batter is in. Bake in a Majestic Range.

Lunch Cake.—Four cups of sugar, three cups of flour, one-half cup of milk, two eggs, two teaspoonfuls of baking powder, one teaspoonful extract of peach. Bake in a Majestic Range.

Gold Cake.—One-half cup of butter, two cups of sugar, three cups of flour, one cup of milk, yolks of ten eggs, one teaspoonful extract of lemon. Bake in a Majestic Range.

Delicate Cake.—One and one-half cups of sugar, one and one-half cups of flour, one cup of corn starch, one-half cup of butter, one-half cup of milk, whites of six eggs, two teaspoonfuls of baking powder; flavor with one-half teaspoonful extract of almond. Bake in a Majestic Range.

Rolled Jelly Cake.—One cup of sugar and two eggs creamed; add two tablespoonfuls of water, one and one-half cups of flour, one teaspoonful of baking powder, one teaspoonful extract of lemon. Bake, in a Majestic Range, in a dripping pan in quick oven; when cool spread with jelly and roll.

Lemon Jelly Cake.—One and one-half cups of sugar, one-half of butter, one-half of milk, two and one-half cups of flour, three eggs, two teaspoonfuls of baking powder, one teaspoonful extract of lemon. Bake in layers in a Majestic Range.

Filling.—One cup of sugar, one egg, grated rind and juice of one lemon, one tablespoonful of water, one teaspoonful of flour. Boil until it thickens; cool and spread between the layers.

Orange Cake.—Make cake part the same as for lemon cake. Bake in a Majestic Range.

Filling.—Whites of two eggs, three cups of sugar, the grated rind and juice of one orange, half the juice of one lemon, two teaspoonfuls extract of orange. Spread between layers.

MAJESTIC RANGE No. 53.

FOR SOFT COAL OR WOOD.

IF FOR HARD COAL OR WOOD No. 53HC.

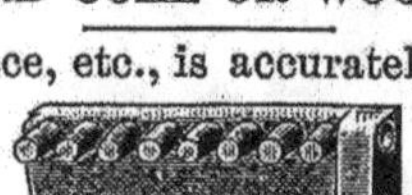

The top cooking surface, etc., is accurately given under No. 52. No doubt readers will have noticed the striking similarity in their constructive features; in fact, one of the strong points we make in recommending our ranges to the public is, that the parts are nearly interchangeable one with the other, as is the case with our "pin extension" water-front in this range. The testimony of users is altogether in its favor.

Price, $56.00.

Prices include delivery on board cars in St. Louis. Freight must be paid by purchasers—the rate varying according to distance—from 25c to $2.00 per 100 lbs.

ICING FOR CAKE.

Boiled Frosting.—One pint of granulated sugar with enough water to dissolve it. Let it boil on a Majestic Range until it threads from the spoon. Beat the whites of two eggs stiff and pour the boiling sugar into it, beating all the time.

Cream Frosting.—Take the whites of two eggs, add an equal measure of cold water, stir into this confectioners' sugar until the right consistency to spread. Flavor with one-half teaspoonful extract of vanilla.

The Best Icing.—One pound of sugar, whites of three eggs; beat the whites until frothy, *not white*, add the sugar gradually with one hand while you beat with the other. Flavor with extract of lemon or almond.

Frosting.—Whites of two eggs, two cups of pulverized sugar, one-half cup corn starch. Beat all together until stiff, and frost the cake while hot.

Soft Icing.—Ten teaspoonfuls of sugar to one egg; beat twenty minutes. Flavor with extract of rose.

Almond Icing.—Three cups of sugar, one pound of almonds, blanched and pounded to a paste; beat the whites of three eggs and stir in the sugar and almonds. Flavor with extract of rose.

Water Icing.—Two cups of sugar, water enough to make a thick paste, a small pinch of cream of tartar. Beat well; if not stiff enough, add more sugar. Flavor with one-half teaspoonful extract of peach.

Chocolate Icing.—Melt three ounces of chocolate in a little water, boil in two cups of sugar, stir in the whites of three well-beaten eggs. Flavor with extract of vanilla.

Orange Cake Frosting.—Yolks of three eggs beaten very light and made stiff with pulverized sugar, one teaspoonful of orange extract; put on the cake while warm.

Gelatine Icing.—Dissolve one tablespoonful gelatine in one-half cup boiling water, and strain; thicken with powdered sugar, and flavor.

Chocolate Icing.—One cup milk; when it comes to a boil, add one cup grated chocolate; when chocolate is dissolved, add one and a half cups pulverized sugar, the yolks of five eggs; after it has been taken from the stove, add one teaspoonful of vanilla.

Crystallization.—Crystallization consists in simply covering the cake while the icing is wet with granulated sugar, plain or pink. Or you can use pink or white sugar, or rock candy crushed. If you wish to crystallize only a portion of the icing, and that in any particular design, first allow the icing to dry, then wash the part you wish crystallized with white of egg or gum water, and cover it with the sugar; then shake off what will not remain on.

MAJESTIC RANGE No. 54.

FOR SOFT COAL OR WOOD.

IF FOR HARD COAL OR WOOD No. 54HC.

Is the last of the series of family ranges, the description of which is fully set forth under No. 52. With its 15-gallon copper reservoir, as shown, it is admirably adapted for small restaurants and hotels, or families who do cooking for twenty to twenty-five persons. As of all our family ranges, we recommend No. 54.

Price, $65.00.

Prices include delivery on board cars in St. Louis. Frieght must be paid by purchasers—the rate varying according to distance—from 25c to $2.00 per 100 lbs.

PASTRY.

In making pastry, care should be taken to handle it as little as possible. The surest way to make a good crust is to chop it together without putting the hands into it. The water, butter or lard should always be cold.

Pie Crust No. 1.—To one pint of flour add one teaspoonful of baking powder, mix in one cup of butter or lard wet with ice water. Will make two pies.

Pie Crust No. 2.—Three cups of flour, one teaspoonful of baking powder, a pinch of salt, one cup of cream, one-half cup of butter. Roll thin.

Pie Crust No. 3.—Four cups of flour, one cup of butter, one cup of lard, a pinch of salt, one cup of water. Chop together, and roll thin.

Pie Crust No. 4.—One quart of flour, one cup of lard, one-half cup of butter, a pinch of salt, ice water to wet. Chop together, and roll thin.

Puff Paste No. 1.—One pound of flour to be mixed with ice water, roll and spread with one pound of butter. Fold over, and roll until butter is all mixed in.

Puff Paste No. 2.—Three cups of flour, one teaspoonful of baking powder, a pinch of salt, one egg; mix flour and egg with ice water; roll out and put on butter in small bits, fold over and roll. Put on ice for twenty minutes. Roll thick.

Apple Pie.—Peel and slice very thin apples enough to fill a pie tin; line pan with crust, put in the apples, cover with sugar and ground cinnamon; cover with crust; bake in a Majestic Range.

Lemon Pie.—Grate the rind of one lemon and use the juice, or two teaspoonfuls of extract of lemon, one cup of sugar, one tablespoonful of butter, two tablespoonfuls of milk, four eggs, mix; pour into pans lined with crust, and bake in a Majestic Range. When done, spread the top with white of one egg, one-half cup of sugar; brown.

Lemon Cream Pie.—Boil one pint of milk, add three teaspoonfuls of corn starch; when boiled, take from range and stir in the yolks of four eggs, two tablespoonfuls of butter, one cup of sugar, the juice of two lemons and rind of one grated; pour into rich crust; bake twenty minutes in a Majestic Range. Whip the whites of four eggs with one cup of sugar. Spread over the top and brown.

Cream Pie No. 1.—Three glasses of milk, three tablespoonfuls of corn starch, yolks of three eggs, two teaspoonfuls extract of lemon, a pinch of salt, boil until thick; pour into a baked crust; whip the whites with one cup of sugar and spread on top. Bake brown in a Majestic Range.

Cream Pie.—Stir to a cream one-half a cup of sugar, one tablespoonful of butter, add two well-beaten eggs, two tablespoonfuls of flour, two cups of milk, two teaspoonfuls extract of orange. Pour into pans lined with crust; bake in a Majestic Range.

Custard Pie.—One quart of milk, five eggs, three tablespoonfuls of sugar, one teaspoonful extract of lemon. Bake in pans lined with plain crust in a Majestic Range.

Chocolate Pie.—Four tablespoonfuls of grated chocolate, one pint of water, yolks of two eggs, two tablespoonfuls of corn starch, six tablespoonfuls of sugar, boil until thick; add one teaspoonful extract of vanilla; bake the crust, pour in the chocolate. Beat the whites of the eggs with one cup of sugar, spread over top, and brown in a Majestic Range.

Marlborough Pie.—Six macaroons, roll fine; one cup of stewed apples, three eggs, one-half pint of cream, one teaspoonful extract of almond, two teaspoonfuls of chopped citron; mix. Line deep pan with crust, pour in the mixture; bake in a Majestic Range.

Cocoanut Pie.—One-half pound of sugar, one-quarter pound of butter, three eggs, one-half pound of grated cocoanut, one teaspoonful extract of rose, mix; pour into pan lined with crust; bake in a Majestic Range.

Pumpkin Pie.—Boil ripe pumpkin until tender, and rub through a colander; one pint of pumpkin, one pint of cream, two eggs, one cup of sugar, one teaspoonful extract of ginger. Pour into pans lined with crust; bake in a Majestic Range.

Sweet Potato Pie.—One pint of mashed sweet potatoes, one cup of sweet milk, one cup of butter, one cup of sugar, four eggs, one nutmeg, one-half teaspoonful extract of lemon. Pour into a pan lined with crust; bake in a Majestic Range.

Mince Pie Meat.—Boil two pounds of good meat tender; chop fine when cold; one-half pound of suet, chopped fine; one tablespoonful of cloves, one of nutmeg, one tablespoonful each extract of cinnamon and ginger, two cups of sugar, one cup of molasses, one cup of wine, one of brandy, two pounds of seeded raisins, two pounds of currants, one pound of citron, chopped fine; two pounds of tart apples, chopped fine; one teaspoonful of salt, one teaspoonful of mace, one of allspice, mix well; put in stone jars and cover. Will keep all winter.

Cherry Pie.—Line the pan with good crust and fill with ripe cherries, stoned; regulate the quantity of sugar you scatter over them by their sweetness. Cover, and bake in a Majestic Range. When cold sift powdered sugar over upper crust.

Blackberry, Raspberry and Plum pies are made in the same way.

Peach Pie.—Line a pie tin with crust, slice the peach and put sugar enough over to sweeten, allow three peach kernels to a pie, add a little water; bake with cross-bars of crust across the top in a Majestic Range. Can be made from canned peaches.

Strawberry Pie.—Put a thin, round, ten-inch wide flat of feuilletage on a baking-sheet; wet the edge, then lay on this a rim of the sauce-paste a third of an inch thick and an inch wide, and make the ends adhere; pick three pints of large and not too ripe strawberries, roll them in fresh butter and powdered sugar, put in the centre of the cake in dome form, wet the rim, and cover with another thin flat of feuilletage; press gently with the thumbs over the rim, trim the edge, baste the surface with egg-white, besprinkle with white granulated sugar, and bake in a moderately heated Majestic Range oven for half an hour without allowing the surface to brown. The flats of paste should be only about an eighth of an inch thick, because this fruit requires no cooking.

Orange Pie.—Grated rind and juice of two oranges, four eggs, four tablespoonfuls sugar, and one of butter; cream the butter and sugar, add the beaten eggs, then the rind and juice of the oranges, and, lastly, the whites beaten to a froth and mixed in lightly. Bake with an under crust in a Majestic Range.

Currant and Raspberry Tart.—Three cups of currants, one cup of raspberries, one and one-half cups of sugar; bake with under and upper crust in a Majestic Range.

Tarts.—Use the best puff paste for tarts, roll thick, and bake in small pans in a Majestic Range; fill with jam, jelly or cream.

Cream Tarts.—Fill tart shells with whipped cream; put a spoonful of jelly on top of cream. Bake in a Majestic Range.

Tart Shells.—Roll thin good puff paste, cut out with a glass; then with a wineglass cut out the center of small ones; lay on top of each other, and bake in a Majestic Range. Fill with jelly or jam.

Almond Tarts.—Beat to a cream the yolks of three eggs and one-quarter of a pound of sugar, add one-half pound of pounded almonds, one teaspoonful extract of almond; put in tart tins lined with paste; bake ten minutes in a Majestic Range.

Cocoanut Tarts.—Dissolve one-half pound of sugar in one-half pint of water, add one pound of grated cocoanut, boil; when cool, add the yolks of three and white of one egg; mix, and pour into tart tins lined with crust; bake in a Majestic Range.

Cheese Cakes.—One cup of grated cocoanut, one cup of milk curds, one cup of cream, yolks of five eggs, one cup of sugar, one teaspoonful extract of almonds; boil until thick; pour into tart tins lined with puff paste; bake ten minutes in a Majestic Range. Orange or lemon can be used in place of cocoanut.

Strawberry Short-Cake.—One quart of flour, two teaspoonfuls of baking powder, a pinch of salt, a tablespoonful of sugar, three tablespoonfuls of butter, and milk to make a soft dough; bake in two layers, one on top of the other, with butter between, in a Majestic Range; when cool, split open with a knife and cover with berries sprinkled with sugar, put other layer of crust on top and cover with berries.

DUMPLINGS.

Apple Dumplings.—Make a soft dough; peel and core tart apples; wrap each apple in the dough, drop in boiling water; eat with sauce.

Steamed Apple Dumplings.—Make a good baking powder crust, peel and core tart apples, fill the cavity in apples with sugar, wrap each in the dough, and steam one hour on a Majestic Range. Serve with butter and sugar sauce.

Baked Apple Dumplings.—Make as for steamed dumplings: put in pan so as not to touch; bake brown in a Majestic Range. Serve with cream sauce,

Peach Dumplings.—Make the same crust as for apple dumplings. Use canned peaches. put a little piece of butter with same and a little sugar, cover in dough, and bake in a Majestic Range. Serve with foaming sauce.

Bar Berries.—Make a crust as for pie, roll out quite thin and cut in rounds with the top of a pint pail, if you are not fortunate enough to have a cutter the requisite size. On these rounds pour a good tablespoonful of this mixture. One cup of stoned and chopped raisins, one piece of citron about the size of a trade dollar. the juice and grated rind of one lemon, one egg, one cup of sugar, and a pinch of salt; mix all well. After putting it on the paste, wrap it together, thus making a sort of little turn over. Do not cut any vent in the dough, but press the edges so firmly together that not a drop can escape. When all are laid side by side in a pan or baking tin, wet them over with milk in which a little sugar is dissolved; this gives them a lovely brown when baked in a Majestic Range.

Boiled Apple Dumplings.—Add to two cups sour milk, one teaspoonful soda, and one of salt, half cup of butter, lard, flour enough to make dough a little stiffer than for biscuit: or make a good baking powder crust; peel and core apples, roll out crust, place apples on dough, fill cavity of each with sugar, encase each apple in coating of the crust, press edges tight together (it is nice to tie a cloth around each one), put into a kettle of boiling water slightly salted, boil half an hour on a Majestic Range, taking care that the water covers the dumplings. They are also very nice steamed. To bake, make in the same way, using a soft dough, place in a shallow pan, bake in a hot oven, and serve with cream and sugar, or place in a pan four or five inches deep (do not have the dumplings touch each other); then pour in hot water, just leaving top of dumplings uncovered. To a pan of four or five dumplings, add one teacupful sugar and half a teacupful butter; bake from half to three-quarters of an hour in a Majestic Range. If water cooks away too much, add more. Serve dumplings on platter and the liquid in sauce-boat for dressing. Fresh or canned peaches may be made in the same way.

DELICIOUS DESSERTS.

DINNER.

SPRING.

Sunday—Brown Top Pudding; Lemon Cakes.
Monday—Almond Custard.
Tuesday—Italian Cream; Pink and White Cake.
Wednesday—Graham Pudding; Lemon Sauce.
Thursday—Fruit Charlotte; White Sponge Cake.
Friday—Malborough Pie.
Saturday—Baked Apple Dumplings.

SUMMER.

Sunday—Strawberry Short Cake; Pine Apple Sherbert.
Monday—Blackberry Pie.
Tuesday—Peach Cottage Pudding; Hard Brandy Sauce.
Wednesday—Roman Punch; Angels' Food.
Thursday—Fruit Cream; Almond Drops.
Friday—Charlotte Russe; Pound Cake.
Saturday—Cherry Pie; Ring Jumbles.

AUTUMN.

Sunday—Peach Ice Cream; Caramel Cake.
Monday—Custard Pie.
Tuesday—Railroad Pudding; White Wine Sauce.
Wednesday—Cocoanut Pie; Sugar Cookies.
Thursday—Apple Fritter; Foaming Sauce.
Friday—Pumpkin Pie.
Saturday—Velvet Blanc Mange.

WINTER.

Sunday—Delmonico Pudding; Hard Brandy Sauce.
Monday—Neapolitan Blanc Mange.
Tuesday—Steamed Fruit Pudding; Wine Jelly.
Wednesday—Tipsy Pudding; Macaroons.
Thursday—Mince Pie.
Friday—Tapioca Cream.
Saturday—Indian Pudding.

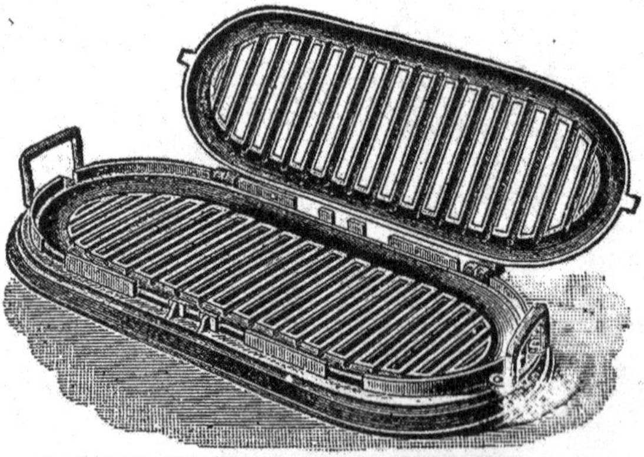

MAJESTIC COMBINATION REVOLVING BROILER.

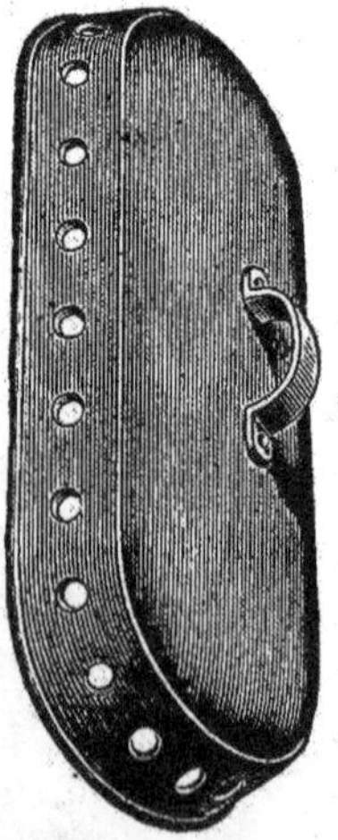

PERFORATED BROILER COVER.

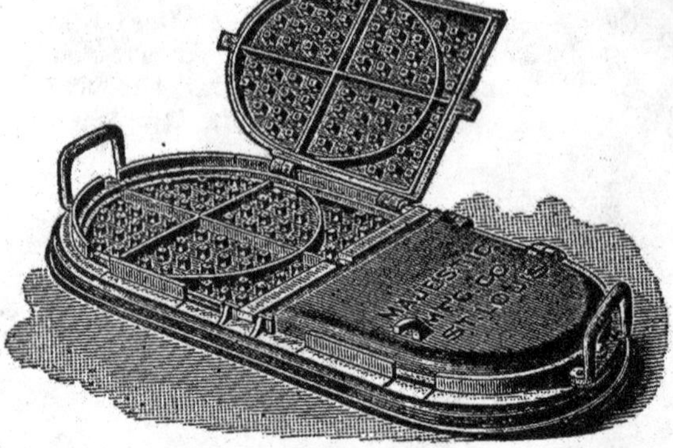

MAJESTIC COMBINATION REVOLVING WAFFLE IRON.

This Broiler can be used on any of our family ranges, and is the essence of simplicity. Both Waffle and Broiler revolve in frame, and are interchangeable. When meats are broiled remove Broiler and put in the waffles. For broiling, place tin cover over the Broiler, close all front drafts, open direct draft damper in range, and air is taken through openings in cover, carrying all smoke and fumes into smoke pipe direct.

Price, complete, $4.50.

MEATS.

Broiled Beefsteak.—Lay a thick, tender steak upon a gridiron well greased with butter or beef suet, over hot coals; when done on one side have ready the warmed platter with a little butter on it, lay the steak, without pressing it, upon the platter with the cooked side down so that the juices which have gathered may run on the platter; quickly place it again on gridiron and cook the other side. When done to liking, put on platter again, spread lightly with butter, season with salt and pepper and place where it will keep warm (over boiling steam is best) for a few moments, but do not let butter become oily. Serve on hot plates. Many prefer to sear on one side, turn immediately and sear the other, and finish cooking, turning often; garnish with fried sliced potatoes, or with browned potato balls the size of a marble, piled at each end of platter. Broil on a Majestic Broiler.

Fried Beefsteak.—When the means to broil are not at hand, the next best method is to heat the frying pan very hot, put in steak previously hacked, let remain a few moments, loosen with knife and turn quickly several times; repeat this, and when done transfer to a hot platter, salt, pepper, and put over it bits of butter; pile the steaks one on top of another, and cover with a hot platter. This way of frying is both healthful and delicate. Or, heat the skillet, trim off the fat from the steak, cut in small bits and set on to fry on a Majestic Range; meanwhile pound steak, then draw the bits of suet to one side and put in the steak, turn quickly over several times so as to sear the outside, take out on a hot platter previously prepared with salt and pepper, dredge well, return to skillet, repeating the operation until the steak is done; dish on a hot platter, covering with another platter, and place where it will keep hot while making the gravy. Place a tablespoon dry flour in the skillet, being sure to have the fat boiling hot, stir until brown and free from lumps (the bits of suet may be left in, drawing them to one side until the flour is browned), pour in about half a pint boiling water (milk or cream is better), stir well, season with pepper and salt, and serve in a gravy tureen. Spread bits of butter over steak and send to table at once. This is more economical, but not so wholesome as broiling.

Beefsteak Smothered in Onions.—Slice the onions thin and drop in cold water; put steak in pan with a little suet. Skim out onions and add to steak, season with pepper and salt, cover tightly and put over the fire. When the juice of the onions has dried up and the meat has browned on one side, remove onions, turn steak, replace onions and fry on a Majestic Range till done, being careful not to burn.

Boiled Corned Beef.—Soak over night if very salt, but if beef is young and properly corned this is not necessary; pour over it cold water enough to cover it well, after washing off the salt. The rule for boiling meats is twenty-five minutes to a pound, but corned beef should be placed on a part of the range where it will simmer, not boil, uninterruptedly from four to six hours, according to the size of the piece. If to be served cold, some let the meat remain in the liquor until cold, and some let tough beef remain in the liquor until the next day, and bring it to the boiling point just before serving. Simmer a brisket or plate-piece until the bones are easily removed, fold over, forming a square or oblong piece, place sufficient weight on top to press the parts closely together and set where it will become cold. This gives a firm, solid piece to cut in slices and is a delightful relish. Boil liquor down, remove the fat, season with pepper or sweet herbs and save it to pour over finely minced scraps and pieces of beef; press the meat firmly into a mold, pour over it the liquor, and place over it a close cover with a weight upon it. When turned from the mold garnish with sprigs of parsley or celery, and serve with fancy pickles or French mustard. Cook on a Majestic Range.

Beef a la Mode.—In a piece of the rump cut deep openings with a sharp knife; put in pieces of pork cut into dice, previously rolled in pepper, salt, cloves and nutmeg. Into an iron stewpan lay pieces of pork, sliced onions, slices of lemon, one or two carrots and a bay leaf; lay the meat on and put over it a piece of bread crust as large as the hand, a half pint wine and a little vinegar, and afterwarde an equal quantity of water or broth, till the meat is half covered; cover the dish close and cook till tender. Then take it out, rub the gravy thoroughly through a sieve, skim off the fat, add some sour cream, return to the stewpan and cook ten minutes on a Majestic Range. Instead of the cream, capers or sliced cucumber pickles can be added to the gravy if preferred, or a handful of grated ginger bread or rye bread. The meat can also be laid for some days before in a spiced vinegar or wine pickle.

Roast Beef.—Take a rib piece or loin roast of seven to eight pounds. Beat it thoroughly all over, lay it in the roasting dish and baste it with melted butter. Put it inside the well-heated Majestic Range oven, and baste frequently with its own fat, which will make it brown and tender. If, when it is cooking fast the gravy is growing too brown, turn a glass of German cooking wine into the bottom of the pan, and repeat this as often as the gravy cooks away. The roast needs about two hours time to be done, and must be brown outside, but inside still a little red. Season with salt and pepper. Squeeze a little lemon juice over it, and also turn the gravy upon it, after skimming off all fat.

Stewed Beef.—Take a piece of the rump, pound it till tender, lay in an iron vessel previously lined with slices of pork and onions, with a few pepper-corns, dredge it with salt, and baste with melted butter. Cover close over a good heat, and when it has fried a nice brown add one pint German cooking wine and as much more good soup stock and stew it till soft on a Majestic Range. Before serving, take out the meat, skim off the fat, add a tablespoon of flour mixed smooth with broth, add gradually still more broth, strain it through a sieve and turn over the previously dished meat. The meat can be laid for some days before in vinegar or in a spiced pickle, or be basted with either occasionally instead of lying in it.

A Brown Stew.—Put on range a rather thick piece of beef with little bone and some fat; four hours before needed pour on just boiling water enough to cover; cover with a close fitting lid, boil gently, and as the water boils away add only just enough from time to time to keep from burning, so that when the meat is tender the water may all be boiled away, as the fat will allow the meat to brown without burning; turn occasionally, brown evenly over a slow fire in a Majestic Range, and make a gravy by stirring flour and water together and adding to the drippings; season with salt an hour before it is done.

Fried Liver.—Cut in thin slices and place on a platter, pour on boiling water and immediately pour it off (this seals the outside, takes away the unpleasant flavor and makes it much more palatable); have ready in skillet on the range some hot lard or beef drippings, or both together, dredge the liver with rolled crackers or dried bread crumbs rolled fine and nicely seasoned with pepper and salt, put in skillet, placing the tin cover on, fry slowly until both sides are dark brown, when the liver will be thoroughly cooked. The time required is about a quarter of an hour on a Majestic Range.

Boiled Mutton with Caper Sauce.—Have ready a pot of boiling water and throw in a handful of salt; wash a leg of mutton and rub salt through it. If it is to be rare, cook about two hours; if well done, three hours or longer, according to size. Boil a pint of milk, thicken with flour well blended, add butter, salt, pepper and two tablespoons of capers, or mint sauce if preferred.

Lamb Stewed with Peas.—Cut the neck or breast in pieces, put it in a stewpan with some salt pork sliced thin and enough water to cover it; cover close and let stew on a Majestic Range until the meat is tender, then skim free from scum, add a quart of green peas shelled, and more hot water if necessary; cover till the peas are done tender, then add a bit of butter rolled in flour, and pepper to taste; let simmer for a few minutes and serve.

Mutton Chops.—Season with salt and pepper, put in skillet, cover closely and fry five minutes, turning over once; dip each chop in beaten egg, then in cracker or bread crumbs, and fry till tender or nicely browned on each side; or put in oven in a dripping pan with a little water, salt and pepper; baste frequently and bake in a Majestic Range until brown. To broil lamb chops, trim neatly, broil over a clear fire, with a Majestic Broiler, season with pepper and salt, and serve with green peas.

Fried Salt Pork.—Cut in rather thin slices, and freshen by letting lie an hour or two in cold water, or milk and water, roll in flour and fry till crisp (if in a hurry pour boiling water on the slices, let stand a few minutes, drain, roll in flour and fry as before); drain off most of the grease from frying pan, stir in while hot one or two tablespoons of flour, half a pint new milk, a little pepper, and salt, if not salt enough already from the meat; let boil and pour into gravy dish. This makes a nice white gravy when properly made. Cook on a Majestic Range.

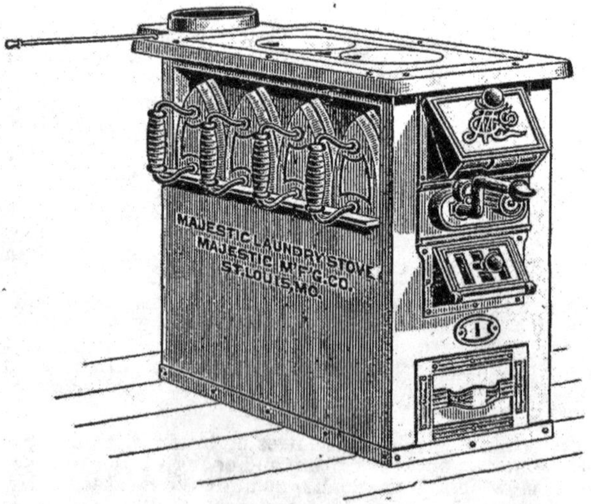

MAJESTIC LAUNDRY STOVE No. 1

Is no doubt the most convenient and economical apparatus that has ever been constructed for laundry purposes. It has space on sides to hold eight sad irons, so arranged that they set closely against fire linings. The stove has open anchor plate, short center, and two 8-inch lids, so that any 8-inch pit or flat-bottom wash boiler may be used on top. If wanted, we connect open top Copper Reservoir with water heater inside of fire box, that will heat 40 gallons of water. Any kind of fuel can be used.

Price, - - $18.50.
With Water Connections, 21.00.

Prices include delivery on board cars in St. Louis. Freight must be paid by purchasers—the rate varying according to distance—from 25c to $2.00 per 100 lbs.

Fried Porksteaks.—Fry like beefsteaks, with pepper and salt, or sprinkle with dry powdered sage if the sausage flavor is liked. Fry on a Majestic Range.

Roast Pork.—A small loin of pork, three tablespoons bread crumbs, one onion, half a teaspoon chopped sage, half teaspoon salt, half teaspoon pepper, one ounce chopped suet, one tablespoon drippings. Separate each joint of the loin with the chopper, and then make an incision with a knife into the thick part of the pork in which to put the stuffing. Prepare the stuffing by mixing the bread crumbs together with the onion, which must have previously been finely chopped. Add to this the sage, pepper, salt and suet, and when all is thoroughly mixed press the mixture snugly into the incision already made in the pork, and sew together the edges of the meat with needle and thread, to confine the stuffing. Grease well a sheet of kitchen paper with drippings, place the loin into this, securing it with a wrapping of twine. Put to bake in a dry baking pan in a brisk Majestic Range oven, basting immediately and constantly as the grease draws out, and roast a length of time, allowing twenty minutes to the pound and twenty minutes longer. Serve with apple sauce or apple fritters.

Veal Loaf.—Chop fine three pounds of leg or loin of veal and three-fourths pound salt pork, chopped finely together; roll one dozen crackers, put half of them in the veal with two eggs, season with pepper and a little salt if needed; mix all together and make into a solid form; then take the crackers that are left and spread smoothly over the outside; bake in a Majestic Range one hour, and eat cold.

Veal or Chicken Pot-Pie.—Put two or three pounds veal (a piece with ribs is good) cut in a dozen pieces in a quart of cold water; make a quart of soda biscuit dough, take two-thirds of dough, roll to a fourth of an inch thick, cut in strips one inch wide by three long; pare and slice six potatoes; boil veal till tender, take out all but three or four pieces, put in two handfuls of potatoes and several strips of dough, then add pieces of veal and dough, seasoning with salt, pepper, and a little butter. until all the veal is in the pot; add boiling water enough to cover, take rest of dough, roll out to size of pot, cut several holes to let steam escape, and place over the whole. Put on a tight lid and boil gently on a Majestic Range twenty or thirty minutes without uncovering.

A Pot Roast.—Take a nice brisket of beef, weighing about four pounds, trim off rough parts; place it in a kettle, over a good fire, on a Majestic Range; brown one side, then turn and brown on the other; then add one pint of boiling water; cover and cook slowly one hour. Add a teaspoonful of salt when the meat is half done. After the water evaporates add no more, as there should be sufficient fat to finish cooking the meat. When the meat is done place it on a heated dish. Drain all the fat but two tablespoonfuls from the pot, and puf it away for frying. To the two tablespoonfuls in the pot add the same quantity of flour. Mix well, and add one pint of water; stir until it boils; season, and pour around the meat.

MAJESTIC RANGE No. 55.

FOR SOFT COAL OR WOOD.

IF FOR HARD COAL OR WOOD 55HC.

This range is the outgrowth of a demand for an intermediate between our 20 and 30-inch ovens; one suited to cook for, say fifty people; and with steam table and hot water connections, 75 to 100 persons. Top cooking surface 34 x 46 inches; six 9-inch lids and key-plate; oven 23 inches wide, 23 inches deep, 16½ inches high; heavy diagonal grates and fire linings, pouch feed fire door, malleable drop oven door, bailed ash pan, "pin extension" water-front, double mantel shelf, nickel-plated protecting bar and brackets, and flue lined with asbestos. Price, $100.00.

Prices include delivery on board cars in St. Louis. Freight must be paid by purchasers—the rate varying according to distance—from 25c to $2.00 per 100 lbs.

Boned Ham.—Having soaked a well-cured ham in tepid water over night, boil it till perfectly tender on a Majestic Range, putting it on in warm water; take up in a wooden tray, let cool, remove bone carefully, press the ham again into shape, return to boiling liquor, remove pot from fire and let the ham remain in it till cool. Cut across and serve cold.

Boiled Ham.—Pour boiling water over it and let stand until cool enough to wash; scrape clean (some have a coarse hair brush on purpose for cleaning hams), put in a thoroughly cleansed boiler with cold water enough to cover; bring to the boiling point and then place on back part of range to simmer steadily for six or seven hours, or till tender when pierced with a fork (if the ham weighs twelve pounds); be careful to keep water at boiling point, and not to allow it to go much above it. Turn the ham once or twice in the water; when done take up and put into a baking pan to skin; dip the hands in cold water, take the skin between the fingers and peel as you would an orange; set in a moderate oven, placing the lean side of the ham downward, and if you like sift over pounded or rolled crackers. Bake one hour in a Majestic Range. The baking brings out a great quantity of fat, leaving the meat much more delicate, and in warm weather it will keep in a dry, cool place a long time; if there is a tendency to mold set it a little while into the oven again. Or, after the ham is boiled and peeled cover with the white of a raw egg, and sprinkle sugar or fine bread crumbs over it; or cover with a regular cake-icing, place in the oven and brown; or, quarter two onions, stick whole allspice and black pepper in the quarters, with a knife make slits in the outside of the ham in which put the onions, place in dripping pan, lay parsley around and bake till nicely browned. Or, after boiling and peeling dust with sugar and pass a hot knife over it until it forms a caramel glaze, and serve without baking. A still nicer way is to glaze with strong meat jelly or any savory jelly at hand, boiled down rapidly (taking great care to prevent burning) until it is like glue. Brush this jelly over the ham when cool and it makes an elegant dish. The nicest portion of a boiled ham may be served in slices, and the ragged parts and odds and ends chopped fine for sandwiches, or by adding three eggs to one pint of chopped ham a delicious omelet may be made. If the ham is very salt it should lie in water over night.

Broiled Ham.—Cut the ham in slices of medium thickness, place on a hot gridiron and broil on a Majestic Broiler until the fat readily flows out and the meat is slightly browned; take from the gridiron with a knife and fork, drop into a pan of cold water, then return to the gridiron, repeat several times, and the ham is done; place in a hot platter, add a few lumps of butter, and serve at once. If too fat trim off a part; it is almost impossible to broil the fat part without burning, but this does not impair the taste. Pickled pork and breakfast bacon may be broiled in the same way.

Delicious Fried Ham.—Place the slices in boiling water and cook till tender; put in frying pan and brown on a Majestic Range, and dish on a platter; fry some eggs by dripping gravy over them until done instead of turning; take up carefully and lay them on the slices of ham.

Fried Veal Cutlets.—Make a batter of half pint of milk, a well-beaten egg, and flour; fry the veal brown in sweet lard or beef drippings, dip it in the batter and fry again till brown; drop some spoonfuls of batter in the hot lard after the veal is taken up, and serve them on top of the meat; put a little flour paste in the gravy with salt and pepper, let it come to a boil and pour it over the whole. The veal should be cut thin, pounded, and cooked nearly an hour in a Majestic Range. Cracker crumbs and eggs may be used instead of batter, but the skillet should then be kept covered, and the veal cooked slowly for half an hour over a moderate fire. If a gravy is wanted sprinkle a little flour in the pan, add salt and pepper and a little water, let come to a boil, and pour over the cutlets; or, pound well, squeeze juice of lemon over the slices, let stand an hour or two, dip in beaten egg and then in fine bread crumbs (if no stale bread is at hand dry slices in a cool oven), plunge at once into hot fat enough to cover. The slices will brown before they are thoroughly cooked, and the pan should be drawn aside to a cooler place to "finish" more slowly.

Fish may be fried in the same way; when done the meat will separate readily from the bone when a knife is inserted. They may be dipped in milk and then in flour, instead of in eggs and bread crumbs; sift salt evenly over the meat or fish just before serving. The bread crumbs should be fine; if coarse, they crumble off with the egg in cooking.

Roast Spare-Rib.—Trim off the rough ends neatly, crack the ribs across the middle, rub with salt and sprinkle with pepper, fold over, stuff with turkey-dressing, sew up tightly, place in dripping pan with pint of water, baste frequently, turning over once so as to bake both sides equally. Bake in a Majestic Range until a rich brown.

Yankee Pork and Beans.—Pick over carefully a quart of beans and let them soak over night; in the morning wash and drain in another water, put on to boil in cold water with half a teaspoon of soda; boil about thirty minutes (when done the skin of a bean will crack if taken out and blown upon), drain, and put in an earthen pot first a slice of pork and then the beans, with two or three tablespoons of molasses. When the beans are in the pot put in the center half or three-fourths of a pound of well-washed salt pork with the rind scored in slices or squares, and uppermost, season with pepper and salt if needed; cover all with hot water, and bake six hours or longer in a moderate oven in a Majestic Range, adding hot water as needed; they can not be baked too long. Keep covered so that they will not burn on the top, but remove cover an hour or two before serving, to brown the top and crisp the pork. This is the Yankee dish for Sunday breakfast. It is often baked the day before, allowed to remain in the oven all night, and browned in the morning. Serve in the dish in which they are cooked, and always have enough left to know the luxury of cold beans, or baked beans warmed over. If salt pork is too robust for the appetites to be served, season delicately with salt, pepper, and a little butter, and roast a fresh spare-rib to serve with them.

MAJESTIC RANGE No. 56.

FOR SOFT COAL OR WOOD.

IF FOR HARD COAL OR WOOD 56HC.

Is made for hotels, restaurants, boarding houses, and camps, for which it is admirably adapted. Top surface 34x55 inches; oven 30 inches wide, 23 inches deep, 17 inches high; eight 9-inch lids or solid plates; diagonal grates, drop oven door, bailed ash pan, double mantel shelf, center flue, one water-front. Price, $135.00.

Prices include delivery on board cars in St. Louis. Freight must be paid by purchasers—the rate varying according to distance—from 25c to $2.00 per 100 lbs.

POULTRY.

Baked Chickens.—Dress the chickens and cut them in two, soak for half an hour in cold water, wipe perfectly dry and put in a dripping-pan, bone side down, without any water; have a hot oven, and, if the chickens are young, half an hour's cooking in a Majestic Range will be sufficient. Take out, and season with butter, salt and pepper; pack one above another as closely as possible, and place in a pan over boiling water, covering them closely—this keeps them moist until served—boil the giblets in a little water, and, after the chickens are taken from the dripping-pan, put into it the water in which giblets were boiled, thicken it, and add the chopped giblets. This manner of baking chickens is fully equal to broiling them.

Baked Spring Chickens.—Cut each of four chickens into seven or nine pieces, wash thoroughly and quickly, and put in a colander to drain, put a half tablespoon each of lard and butter into a dripping-pan, lay in the pieces, and add half a pint hot water; place in Majestic Range oven and bake half an hour, turn, taking care that they get only to a light brown, and, just before taking up, add salt and pepper to taste; when done, take out in a dish and keep hot. To make the gravy, add a half pint or more of water, set the dripping-pan on the range, and add one tablespoon flour mixed with half cup of cream or milk, stirring slowly, adding a little of the mixture at a time, Let cook thoroughly, stirring constantly to prevent burning, and to make the gravy nice and smooth; season more if necessary.

Baked Chicken with Parsnips.—Wash, scrape and quarter parsnips, and parboil for twenty minutes; prepare a young chicken by splitting open at back, place in a dripping-pan, skin side up, lay parsnips around the chicken, sprinkle with salt and pepper, and add a lump of butter the size of an egg, or two or three slices of good pickled pork; put enough water in pan to prevent burning, place in Majestic Range oven and bake until chickens and parsnips are done to a delicate brown; serve chicken separately on a platter, pouring the gravy in the pan over the parsnips.

Chicken Croquettes.—Boil two fowls weighing five pounds each till very tender, mince fine, add one pint cream, half pound butter, salt and pepper to taste; shape oval in a jelly glass or mold. Fry in lard like doughnuts until brown on a Majestic Range.

Breaded Chicken.—Cut a tender chicken into seven pieces, as if for frying, roll in beaten yolks of two eggs, then in finely grated bread crumbs, seasoned with chopped parsley, pepper and salt; place in dripping-pan, dot the pieces with bits of butter (one tablespoon in all), add a little water, bake slowly in a Majestic Range, basting often. When done, take out chicken and make gravy in the pan by adding a mixture of flour and butter, make smooth by stirring. Add either cream or milk to make sufficient gravy, which season to taste.

Broiled Chickens or Quails.—Cut a chicken open on the back, lay on the meat-board and pound until it will lie flat, place on Majestic Broiler and broil until a nice brown, but do not burn. It will take twenty or thirty minutes to cook thoroughly, and it will cook much better to cover with a pie-tin held down with a weight, so that all parts of the chicken may lie close to the broiler. While the chicken is broiling, put the liver, gizzard and heart in a stew-pan and boil in a pint of water until tender, chop fine and add flour, butter, pepper, salt, and stir a cup of sweet cream to the water in which they were boiled; when the chicken is done, dip in this gravy while hot, lay it back on the broiler a minute, put it in the gravy and let boil for half a minute, and send to the table hot. Cook quails in the same way.

Dressing for Chicken or Beef.—Boil potatoes, mash as if for the table, except that they should be less moist, stuff the chicken or roast with this, and bake as ordinarily in a Majestic Range; for ducks, add onions chopped fine; if the bread-dressing is wanted too, it may be laid in the corner of the pan.

Fricasseed Chicken.—Cut up and put on to boil, skin side down, on a Majestic Range in a small quantity of water, season with salt, pepper, and slices of an onion if liked; stew gently until tender, remove chicken, add a half pint of cream or milk to gravy, and thicken with butter and flour rubbed smoothly together (adding a little of the gravy to soften and help mix them), let boil two or three minutes, add a little chopped parsley, and serve. Or, first fry the chicken brown in a little hot lard on a Majestic Range, take out chicken, add a tablespoon flour, and let cook a minute, stirring constantly; add a pint of water (or stock, if at hand), a little vinegar or Worcestershire sauce, season with salt and pepper; when it has boiled, remove from fire, strain, add the beaten yolk of an egg, pour over the chicken and serve. Or, put chicken in sauce-pan with barely enough water to cover, stew gently until tender; have a frying-pan prepared with a few slices of salt pork, drain chicken, and fry with pork on a Majestic Range until it is a fine, rich brown; take chicken and bits of pork from the pan, pour in the broth, thicken with brown flour, mixed smooth with a little water, and season with pepper; now put chicken and pork back into gravy, let simmer a few minutes, and serve very hot.

English Roast Turkey.—Kill several days before cooking, prepare in the usual manner, stuff with bread-crumbs (not using the crusts) rubbed fine, moistened with butter and two eggs, seasoned with salt, pepper, parsley, sage, thyme or sweet marjoram; sew up, skewer, and place to roast in a rack within a dripping-pan in a Majestic Range; spread with bits of butter, turn and baste frequently with butter, pepper, salt and water; a few minutes before it is done glaze with the white of an egg; dish the turkey, pour off most of the fat, add the chopped giblets and the water in which they were boiled, thicken with flour and butter rubbed together, stir in the dripping-pan, let boil thoroughly and serve in a gravy-boat. Garnish with fried oysters, and serve with celery sauce and stewed gooseberries. Choose a turkey weighing from eight to ten pounds. If it becomes too brown, cover with buttered paper.

Chickens for Lunch.—Split a young chicken down the back, wash and wipe dry, season with salt and pepper. Put in a dripping-pan, and place in a moderate Majestic Range oven; bake three-quarters of an hour, This is much better for traveling lunch than when seasoned with butter.

Chicken Pot-pie.—Cut up a chicken and place on a Majestic Range in hot water enough to cover, and take care that it does not cook dry; while boiling cut off a slice from bread dough, add a small lump of lard, and mix up like light biscuit, roll, cut out with cake-cutter, and set by range to rise; wash and pare potatoes of moderate size, and add them when chicken is almost done; when potatoes begin to boil, season with salt and pepper, add dumplings and season again. See that there is water enough to keep from burning, cover very tightly, and do not take cover off until dumplings are done. They will cook in half an hour, and may be tested by lifting one edge of the lid, taking out a dumpling, and breaking it open. Or the dumplings may be placed in steamer over cold water, taking care to leave some of the holes in steamer open—as, if all are covered by the dumplings, the steam will not be admitted, and they will not cook well. If there are too many dumplings to lie on bottom without covering all holes, attach them to the side and upper edge of steamer by wetting dough and pressing it to the edge. When done, remove to vegetable dish and pour hot gravy over them. Dish potatoes by themselves, and chickens and dumplings together. Make gravy by mixing two level tablespoons flour and a little butter together, and stir into the broth remaining in pot slowly, add more boiling water if needed, and season with salt and pepper. Or, make dumplings with one pint sour milk, two well-beaten eggs, half teaspoon soda (mixed in part of the flour), and flour enough to make as stiff as can be stirred with a spoon; or baking powder and sweet milk may be used. Drop in by spoonfuls, cover tightly, and boil on a Majestic Range, as above. A pot-pie may be made from a good boiling piece of beef; if too much grease arises, skim off.

Chicken Pie.—Cut up two young chickens, place on a Majestic Range in hot water enough to cover (as it boils away add more, so as to have enough for the pie and for gravy to serve with it), boil until tender; line the sides of a four or six quart pan with a rich baking powder or soda biscuit dough quarter of an inch thick, put in part of the chicken, season with salt, pepper and butter, lay in a few thin strips or squares of dough, add the rest of chicken and season as before; some add five or six fresh eggs, or a few new potatoes in their season; season liquor in which the chickens are boiled with butter, salt and pepper, add a part of it to the pie, cover with crust a quarter of an inch thick with a hole in the center the size of a tea cup. Keep adding the chicken liquor as needed, since the fault of most chicken pies is that they are too dry. There can scarcely be too much gravy. Bake one hour in a moderate oven.

Veal pies are similarly made, omitting eggs, and using two or three pounds veal to a quart of dough. Add to the liquor left in pot a tablespoon of butter mixed with flour to a paste, season with pepper and salt for gravy, adding water if needed.

MAJESTIC RANGE No. 57.

FOR SOFT COAL OR WOOD.

IF FOR HARD COAL OR WOOD 57HC.

Is designed to supply the demands of people who have large families, or who entertain and do cooking for large numbers. It has two ovens, each 15 inches wide, 21 inches deep, 13 inches high, with large warming oven under each. One fire, with our regulating dampers governing the temperature in either oven, to suit the wants of the cook. Top surface 32x53 inches; six 8-inch lids, and key plates, double mantel shelf, diagonal grates, bailed ash pan, and horse-shoe water-back. Price, $110.00.

Prices include delivery on board cars in St. Louis. Freight must be paid by purchasers—the rate varying according to distance—from 25c to $2.00 per 100 lbs.

GAME.

Quail on Toast.—Dry-pick them, singe them with paper, cut off heads, and legs at first joint, draw, split down the back, soak in salt and water for five or ten minutes, drain and dry with a cloth, lard them with bacon or butter and rub salt over them, place on Majestic Broiler and turn often, dipping two or three times into melted butter; broil about twenty minutes. Have ready as many slices of buttered toast as there are birds, and serve a bird, breast upward, on each slice.

Broiled Pheasant or Prairie Chicken.—Scald and skin, cut off the breast and cut the rest up in joints, being careful to remove all shot; put in hot water all except the breast (which will be tender enough without parboiling), and boil until it can be pierced with fork; take out, rub over salt, pepper and butter, and broil with breast over brisk fire on a Majestic Broiler; place a lump of butter on each piece and set all in the oven a few minutes. For breakfast serve on fried mush; for dinner, on toast with a bit of currant jelly over each piece. It may be served with toast cut in pieces about two inches square, over which pour gravy made by thickening the liquor in which the birds were boiled, with a little butter and flour rubbed together and stirred in while boiling. Squirrels may be prepared the same way.

Broiled Quail.—Split through the back and broil over a hot fire on a Majestic Broiler, basting frequently with butter. When done place a bit of butter on each piece and set in a Majestic Range oven a few moments to brown. Serve on pieces of toast with currant jelly. Plovers are cooked in the same way. Pigeons should be first parboiled and then broiled.

Prairie Chickens.—Cut out all shot, wash thoroughly but quickly, using some soda in the water, rinse and dry, fill with dressing, sew up with cotton thread, and tie down the legs and wings; place in a steamer over hot water till done, remove to a dripping pan, cover with butter, sprinkle with salt and pepper, dredge with flour, place in a Majestic Range oven and baste with the melted butter until a nice brown. Serve with either apple sauce, cranberries or currant jelly.

Roast Duck.—Ducks are dressed and stuffed in the same manner as above. Young ducks should roast from twenty-five to thirty minutes; full-grown for an hour or more with frequent basting. Some prefer them underdone, served very hot, but thorough cooking will prove more generally palatable. Serve with currant jelly, apple sauce and green peas. If old, parboil before roasting.

Place the remains of a cold roast duck in a stew pan with a pint of gravy and a little sage, cover closely and let it simmer for half an hour on a Majestic Range; add a pint of boiled green peas, stew a few minutes, remove to a dish, and pour over it the gravy and peas.

Roast Quails.—Pluck and dress like chickens, wipe clean, and rub both inside and out with salt and pepper; stuff with any good dressing and sew up with fine thread; spread with butter and place in a Majestic Range oven with a good steady heat, turning and basting often with hot water seasoned with butter, salt and pepper; bake three-quarters of an hour. When about half done add a little hot water to the pan, and it is well to place a dripping pan over them to prevent browning too much. Add to the gravy flour and butter rubbed together, and water if needed.

Roast Goose.—The goose should not be more than eight months old, and the fatter the more tender and juicy the meat. A "green" goose (four months old) is the choicest. Kill at least twenty-four hours before cooking; cut the neck close to the back, beat the breast-bone flat with a rolling pin, tie the wings and legs securely, and stuff with the following mixture: Three pints bread crumbs, six ounces butter, or part butter and part salt pork, two chopped onions, one teaspoon each of sage, black pepper and salt. Do not stuff very full, and stitch openings firmly together to keep flavor in and fat out. If the goose is not fat, lard it with salt pork, or tie a slice on the breast. Place in a baking pan with a little water, and baste frequently with salt and water (some add onion and some vinegar), turning often so that the sides and back may all be nicely browned. When nearly done baste with butter and a little flour. Bake in a Majestic Range two hours or more if old. When done take from the pan, pour off the fat, and to the brown gravy left add the chopped giblets which have previously been stewed till tender, together with the water they were boiled in; thicken with a little flour and butter rubbed together, bring to a boil, and serve with currant jelly. Apple sauce and onion sauce are proper accompaniments to roast goose.

Reed Birds.—Roasting by suspending on the little wire which accompanies the roaster is the best method; turn and baste frequently, or wash and peel with as thin a paring as possible large potatoes of equal size, cut a deep slice off one end of each and scoop out a part of the potato; drop a piece of butter into each bird, pepper and salt, and put it in the hollows made in the potatoes; put on as covers the pieces cut off, and clip the other end for them to stand on. Set in a baking pan upright with a little water to prevent burning, bake slowly in a Majestic Range, and serve in the dish in which they are baked. Or, boil in a crust like dumplings.

Rabbits.—Rabbits, which are in the best condition in mid-winter, may be fricasseed like chicken in white or brown sauce. To make a pie, first stew till tender and make like chicken pie. To roast, stuff with a dressing made of bread crumbs, chopped salt pork, thyme, onion, and pepper and salt; sew up, rub over with a little butter, or pin on it a few slices of salt pork, add a little water in the pan, and baste often. Serve with mashed potatoes and currant jelly. Bake in a Majestic Range.

Snipe.—Snipe are best roasted with a piece of pork tied to the breast, or they may be stuffed and baked in a Majestic Range.

MAJESTIC RANGE No. 58.
FOR SOFT COAL OR WOOD.

IF FOR HARD COAL OR WOOD 58HC.

Has two ovens, each 17 inches wide, 23 inches deep, 13 inches high, with center flue one fire; center plate with reducing ring, balance solid or open, with lids as desired Top cooking surface 34 x 62 inches, double mantel shelf, lower warming ovens, baile ash pan, heavy diagonal grates and fire linings, pin extension waterback. End flu lined with pure asbestos board. For parts in steel, malleable and gray iron see page 11.

Price, $135.0

Prices Include delivery on board cars in St. Louis. Freight must be paid by purchasers the rate varying according to distance—from 25c to $2.00 per lbs.

FISH.

Baked Fish.—Clean, rinse, and wipe dry a white fish, or any fish weighing three or four pounds, rub the fish inside and out with salt and pepper, fill with a stuffing made like that for poultry but drier; sew it up and put in a hot pan with some drippings and a lump of butter, dredge with flour, and lay over the fish a few thin slices of salt pork or bits of butter; bake an hour and a half in a Majestic Range, basting occasionally.

Baked Shad.—Open and clean the fish, cut off head (or not as preferred) cut out the backbone from the head to within two inches of the tail and fill with the following mixture: Soak stale bread in water, squeeze dry; cut a large onion in pieces, fry in butter, chop fine, add the bread, two ounces of butter, salt, pepper, and a little parsley or sage; heat thoroughly, and when taken from the fire add two yolks of well-beaten eggs; stuff, and, when full, wind the fish several times with tape, place in baking pan in a Majestic Range, baste slightly with butter, and cover the bottom of pan with water. Serve with the following sauce:

Sauce.—Reduce the yolks of two hard-boiled eggs to a smooth past add two tablespoons olive oil, half teaspoon mustard, and pepper an vinegar to taste.

Baked Salmon, Trout or Pickerel.—Clean thoroughly, wipe carefully, and lay in a dripping pan with hot water enough to prevent scorching (a perforated tin sheet or rack fitting loosely in the pan, or several muffin rings may be used to keep the fish from the bottom of the pan, and the fish may be made to form a circle by tying head and tail together); bake slowly in a Majestic Range, basting often with butter and water. When done have ready a cup of sweet cream into which a few spoons of hot water have been poured, stir in two tablespoons melted butter and a little chopped parsley, and heat in a vessel of boiling water; add the gravy from the dish and boil up once. Place the fish in a hot dish and pour over the sauce.

Codfish a la Mode.—Teacup codfish picked up fine, two cups mashed potatoes, one pint cream or milk, two eggs well beaten, half teacup butter, salt and pepper; mix well, bake in baking dish from twenty to twenty-five minutes in a Majestic Range.

Boiled Fish.—To boil a fish fill with a rich dressing of rolled crackers seasoned with butter, pepper, salt and sage, wrap it in a well-floured cloth, tie closely with twine or sew, and place in well-salted boiling water. Place where it will simmer from eight to ten minutes to the pound, on a Majestic Range, according to size and thickness of fish.

Boiled Salt Mackerel.—After freshening wrap in a cloth and simmer for fifteen minutes on a Majestic Range; it will be almost done as soon as the water reaches the boiling point; remove, lay on it two hard-boiled eggs sliced, pour over it drawn butter and trim with parsley leaves. Boiling salt fish hardens it.

Boiled White Fish.—Dress the fish nicely and cover in fish kettle with boiling water seasoned well with salt; remove the scum as it rises, and simmer, allowing from eight to ten minutes time to every pound; when about half done add a little vinegar or lemon juice, take out, drain, and dish carefully, pouring over it drawn butter; or garnish with sprigs of parsley, and serve with egg sauce. Cook on a Majestic Range.

Broiled White Fish.—Clean, split down the back, and let stand in salted water for several hours; wipe dry and place on a well-greased gridiron over hot coals, sprinkling with salt and pepper. Put flesh side down at first, and when nicely browned turn carefully on the other. Cook on a Majestic Range for twenty or thirty minutes, or until nicely browned on both sides.

Brook Trout.—Wash and drain in a colander a few minutes, split nearly to the tail, flour nicely and put in pan, which should be hot but not burning; throw in a little salt to prevent sticking, and do not turn untii brown enough for the table. Trout are nice fried with slices of salt pork. Cook on a Majestic Range.

Codfish Balls.—Soak codfish cut in pieces about an hour in lukewarm water, remove skin and bones, pick to small pieces and return to range in cold water. As soon as it begins to boil change the water and bring to a boil again. Have ready potatoes boiled tender, well mashed and seasoned with butter. Mix thoroughly with the potatoes half the quantity of codfish while both are still hot, form into flat, thick cakes or round balls, fry in hot lard or drippings on a Majestic Range, or dip in hot fat like doughnuts. The addition of a beaten egg before making into balls renders them lighter. Cold potatoes may be used by reheating, adding a little cream and butter and mixing while hot.

Fried Fish.—Clean thoroughly, cut off the head, and, if large, cut out the backbone, and slice the body crosswise into five or six pieces; dip in Indian meal or wheat flour, or in a beaten egg, and then in bread crumbs (trout and perch should never be dipped in meal), put into a thick-bottomed skillet, skin side uppermost, with hot lard or drippings fry slowly on a Majestic Range and turn when a light brown. The roe and the backbone if previously removed may be cut up and fried with the other pieces. A better way is to dredge the pieces in the flonr, brush with beaten egg, roll in bread crumbs and fry in hot lard or drippings enough to completely cover them. If the fat is very hot the fish will not absorb it and will be delicately cooked. When brown on one side turn over in the fat and brown the other, and when done let them drain. Slices of large fish may be cooked in the same way. Serve with tomato sauce or slices of lemon.

Pan-Fish.—Place in pan with heads together and fill spaces with smaller fish; when ready to turn put a plate over, drain off fat, invert pan, and the fish will be left unbroken on the plate. Put the lard back in the pan, and when hot slip back the fish, and when the other side is brown drain, turn on plate as before, and slide them on the platter to go to the table. Cook on a Majestic Range.

EGGS.

To Make Omelet.—Beat the yolks lightly; then add the milk, the salt, pepper, and flour if any is used, and lastly the whites beaten to a stiff froth. Have the skillet as hot as it can be without scorching the butter; put in a tablespoon of butter and pour in the omelet, which should at once begin to bubble and rise in flakes. Slip under it a thin, broad-bladed knife, and every now and then raise it up to prevent burning. As soon as the under side is hard enough to hold together, and the eggs begin to "set," fold over, shake the skillet so as to entirely free the omelet, carefully slide it on a hot platter and serve at once. It should be cooked in from three to five minutes. To bake an omelet place in the frying-pan on top of range until it begins to "set" in the middle, then place in a rather hot Majestic Range oven; when slightly browned, fold if you like, or turn a hot dish on top of the pan, upset the latter with a quick motion, and so dish the omelet with the under side uppermost. It should be baked in from five to ten minutes. Where a large quantity of eggs are used, instead of making into one large omelet, divide and make several, sending each to the table as soon as done. Three eggs make a good-sized omelet. Ham, chicken and all kinds of meat omelets are made by chopping the meat fine and placing between the folds before dishing. In making vegetable (asparagus, tomatoes, cauliflower, etc.) omelets cook the vegetables as if for the table; place them in the center of the omelet just before folding.

For a plain, easily-made omelet take three tablespoons milk and a pinch of salt for each egg; beat the eggs lightly for three or four minutes, pour them into a hot pan in which a piece of butter the size of a walnut has just been melted, cook three or four minutes, fold over and serve at once. Some scald a little parsley, pour off the water, chop it, and mix with the omelet just before pouring into the pan. Old cheese grated and added to a plain omelet is a favorite dish. To make a bread omelet remove all crust from a large slice of light, white bread, moisten with sweet milk, rub through a sieve, add to the yolks, beat very thoroughly, and season with salt and pepper to taste, adding beaten whites last.

Washington Omelet.—Let one teacup milk come to a boil, pour it over one teacup bread crumbs and let stand a few minutes. Break six eggs into a bowl; stir (not beat) till well mixed; then add the milk and bread; mix; season with salt and pepper and pour into a hot skillet, in which a large tablespoon of butter had been melted; fry slowly, cut in squares, turn, fry a delicate brown on a Majestic Range; serve at once.

Curried Eggs.—Slice two onions and fry in butter, add a tablespoon curry powder and one pint good broth or stock; stew till onions are quite tender, add a cup of cream thickened with arrowroot or rice flour, simmer a few moments on a Majestic Range, then add eight or ten hard-boiled eggs, cut in slices and beat them well, but do not boil.

MAJESTIC RANGE No. 59.

FOR SOFT COAL OR WOOD.

IF FOR HARD COAL OR WOOD 59HC.

Has two ovens, each 20 inches wide, 23 inches deep, 13 inches high, with center flues, one fire; center plate with reducing ring, balance solid or open, with lids as desired. Top cooking surface 34 x 70 inches, double mantel shelf, lower warming ovens, bailed ash pan, heavy diagonal grates and fire linings, pin extension waterback. End flue lined with pure asbestos board. For parts in steel, malleable and gray iron see page 11.

Price, $150.00.

CHARCOAL BROILER, 18 INCH.

Has extended cheek pieces and apron, large coal bin underneath, malleable iron broiler bars, open fire grates or solid base as preferred. The broiler proper is 18 inches wide, 30 inches deep; total height 54 inches. It is lined inside with pure asbestos board.

Price, $50.00.

CHARCOAL BROILER, 24 INCH.

Is made precisely the same as the 18-inch, except in size. It is 24 inches wide, 30 inches deep, 54 inches high.

Price, 24-inch, $65.00.
Price, 36-inch, $80.00.

Prices include delivery on board cars in St. Louis. Freight must be paid by purchasers—the rate varying according to distance—from 25c to $2.00 per 100 lbs.

Boiled Eggs.—Put them on in cold water, and when it has boiled on a Majestic Range the eggs will be done, the whites being soft and digestible, as they are not when put on in boiling water.

Escaloped Eggs.—Moisten bread crumbs with milk or meat broth, place a layer of this in a well-buttered dish, slice some hard-boiled eggs, and dip each slice in a thick drawn butter sauce to which a well-beaten egg has been added; put a layer of them upon the crumbs, then a slight layer of minced ham, veal or chicken, then bread, etc., finishing with dry, sifted bread crumbs; bake until well heated in a Majestic Range. Or, mix equal parts minced ham and fine bread crumbs, season with salt, pepper and melted butter, adding milk to moisten till quite soft; half fill buttered gem pans or small patty pans with this mixture, and break an egg carefully upon the top of each, dust with salt and pepper, sprinkle finely powdered crackers over all, set in the oven and bake eight minutes. Serve immediately.

Frizzled Ham and Eggs.—Take bits of either boiled or fried ham, chop fine and place in a skillet prepared with butter or beef drippings; take four to six well-beaten eggs, pour over ham, and when heated through season well with pepper and salt; stir together, cook until done brown on a Majestic Range, and turn over without stirring.

Poached Eggs.—Break and drop them one at a time in salted water, to which some add a small lump of butter; some say drop in when simmering, others when boiling, not letting it boil again after putting in the eggs; others have water boiling, salt, then place it where it will stop boiling, drop in eggs and let simmer gently till done on a Majestic Range. Always take great care in keeping the yolk whole. To preserve the egg round, muffin rings may be placed in the water, or stir with a spoon and drop in the eddy thus made, stirring till egg is cooked. To serve them toast squares of bread three-quarters of an inch thick, put a very little melted butter upon each slice, place on a heated platter, lay an egg on each square, and sprinkle with pepper and salt. Some put a bit of butter on each egg. Serve with Worcester sauce if desired. Some poach eggs in milk, serving them in sauce dishes with some of the milk, and seasoning with pepper and salt.

Scrambled Eggs.—In a deep earthen pie plate, warm sweet milk, allowing two tablespoons to each egg (or less, with a large number of eggs), add a bit of butter size of a walnut, and a little salt and pepper. When nearly to boiling point drop in the eggs, broken one at a time in a saucer; with a spoon or thin-bladed knife gently cut the eggs, and scrape the mixture up from the bottom of the plate as it cooks. If it begins to cook dry and fast at the bottom move the dish back instantly, for success depends wholly on cooking gently and evenly, proportions being of secondary importance. Take from range before it has quite all thickened, and continue turning it up from the bottom of the dish a moment longer. If served in another dish (it keeps warmer served in same) have it well heated. The mixture should be in large flakes of mingled white and yellow, and as delicate as baked custard. Some prefer them scrambled without the milk. Cook on a Majestic Range.

VEGETABLES.

Dry Lima Beans.—Wash one quart of dry lima beans in two warm waters, soak three hours, drain, and put on Majestic Range to cook in enough boiling water to cover them; cover pot with tin lid, adding more hot water as it boils away, boiling rapidly for one and a half hours, when there should be only water enough to come up to top of the beans—just sufficient to make a nice dressing. Five minutes before taking up, season with salt and pepper, and stir in a dressing made of one tablespoon each of flour and butter, rubbed together until smooth. This is a delicious dish.

String Beans.—String, snap and wash two quarts beans, boil on Majestic Range, in plenty of water about fifteen minutes, drain off and put on again in about two quarts boiling water; boil an hour and a half, and add salt and pepper just before taking up, stirring in one and a half tablespoons butter rubbed into two tablespoons flour and half pint sweet cream.

Or, boil a piece of salted pork on Majestic Range one hour, then add beans and boil an hour and a half. For shelled beans boil half an hour in water enough to cover, and dress as above.

Stewed Carrots.—Take any quantity desired, divide the carrots lengthwise, and boil on Majestic Range until perfectly tender, which will require from one to two hours. When done, have ready a sauce-pan with one or two tablespoons butter, and small cup cream; slice the carrots very thin, and put in the sauce-pan; add salt and pepper, and let stew ten or fifteen minutes, stirring gently once or twice, and serve in a vegetable dish. Some add more milk or cream; when done skim out carrots, and to the cream add a little flour thickening, or the beaten yolks of one or two eggs. When it boils pour over the carrots and serve. Carrots may also be boiled with meat like turnips or parsnips, but they take longer to cook than either.

Stewed Corn.—Cut with a sharp knife through the center of every row of grains, and cut off the outer edge; then with the back of the blade push out the yellow eye, with the rich, creamy center of the grain, leaving the hull on the cob. To one quart of this add half a pint rich milk, and stew until cooked in a covered tin pail, in a kettle one-third full of boiling water; then add salt, white pepper, and two or three ounces butter; allow two hours for cooking on a Majestic Range; it seems a long time, but there is no danger of burning, and it requires no more attention than to stir it occasionally and to keep good the supply of water. If drier than liked, add more milk or cream. Or, after cutting corn from the cob, boil the cobs ten or fifteen minutes and take out and put corn in same water; when tender, add a dressing of milk, butter, pepper and salt, and just before serving stir in beaten eggs, allowing three eggs to a dozen ears of corn.

Heidelberg Cabbage.—Select two small, solid heads of hard red cabbage; divide them in halves from crown to stem; lay the split side down, and cut downwards in thin slices. The cabbage will then be in narrow strips or shreds. Put into a saucepan a tablespoon of clean drippings, butter, or any nice fat; when fat is hot, put in cabbage a teaspoon of salt, three tablespoons vinegar (if the latter is very strong use but two), and one onion, in which three or four cloves have been stuck, buried in the middle; boil two hours and a half on a Majestic Range; if it becomes too dry and is in danger of scorching add a very little water. This is very nice.

Fried Cabbage.—Cut the cabbage very fine, on a slaw cutter, if possible; salt and pepper, stir well, and let stand five minutes. Have an iron kettle smoking hot, drop one tablespoon lard into it, then the cabbage, stirring briskly until quite tender; send to table immediately. One-half cup sweet cream and three tablespoons vinegar—the vinegar added after the cream has been well stirred, and after taking from the Majestic Range, is an agreeable change. When properly done an invalid can eat it without injury, and there is no offensive odor from cooking.

Dandelions.—They are fit for use until they blossom. Cut off the leaves, pick over carefully, wash in several waters, put into boiling water, boil one hour, drain well, add salted boiling water, and boil two hours on a Majestic Range; when done, turn into a colander and drain, season with butter, and more salt if needed, and cut with a knife; or boil with a piece of salt pork, omitting the butter in the dressing.

Boiled or Fried Onions.—Wash and peel, boil ten minutes, pour off this water, again add boiling water, boil a few minutes and drain a second time; pour on boiling water, add salt and boil for one hour on a Majestic Range; place in a colander, turn a saucer over them and press firmly to drive off all the water; place in a dish and add butter and pepper. Or, about half an hour before they are done, turn a pint of milk into the water in which they are boiling, and, when tender, season as above. Old onions require two hours to boil. To fry onions, slice and boil ten minutes each time in three waters, drain, fry in butter or beef drippings, stir often, season, and serve hot.

Potatoes Boiled or Baked in Jackets.—Wash clean (a brush is the best implement for cleaning potatoes), cut off the ends, let stand in cold water a few hours, put into boiling water, the larger ones first, and then in a short time adding the rest, cover, and keep boiling constantly; after fifteen minutes throw in another handful of salt and boil another fifteen minutes on a Majestic Range; try with a fork, and if it does not quite run through the potato, they are done. (This is called "leaving a bone in them.") Drain, take to door or window and shake in open air to make them mealy; return to range and allow to stand uncovered for a moment. Or, when washed, bake in a moderate oven fifty minutes; or, place in a steamer half an hour over water kept constantly boiling; serve immediately; or, wash and peel medium-sized ones and bake in pan with roast meat, basting often with the drippings.

Boiled Corn.—Put the well-cleaned ears in salted boiling water, boil an hour on a Majestic Range, or boil in the husk for the same time, remove husks and serve immediately. Corn thoroughly cooked is a wholesome dish.

Hominy.—Soak one quart of ground hominy over night, put over the fire in a tin pail, set in boiling water with water enough to cover, boil gently for five hours on a Majestic Range, as it can not be hurried. After the grains begin to soften on no account stir it. The water put in at first ought to be enough to finish it, but if it proves too little, add more carefully, as too much makes it sloppy. Salt just before taking from the range, as too early salting makes it dark. If properly done, the grains will stand out snowy and well done, but round and separate.

Boiled Cauliflower.—To each half gallon water allow heaped tablespoon salt; choose close and white cauliflower, trim off decayed outside leaves, and cut stock off flat at bottom; open flower a little in places to remove insects which generally are found about the stalk, and let cauliflowers lie with heads downward in salt and water for two hours previous to dressing them, which will effectually draw out all vermin. Then put into boiling water, adding salt in above proportion, and boil briskly for fifteen or twenty minutes over a good fire on a Majestic Range, keeping the saucepan uncovered. The water should be well skimmed. When cauliflowers are tender, take up, drain, and if large enough place upright in dish; serve with plain melted butter, a little of which may be poured over the flowers, or a white sauce may be used made as follows:

Put butter size of an egg into the saucepan, and when it bubbles stir in a scant half teacup of flour; stir well with an egg whisk until cooked; then add two teacups of thin cream, some pepper and salt. Stir it over the fire until perfectly smooth. Pour the sauce over the cauliflower and serve. Many let the cauliflower simmer in the sauce a few moments before serving. Cauliflower is delicious served as a garnish around spring chicken, or with fried sweetbreads, when the white sauce should be poured over both. In this case it should be made by adding the cream, flour, and seasoning to the little grease (half a teaspoon) that is left after frying the chickens or sweetbreads.

Delicate Cabbage.—Remove all defective leaves, quarter and cut as for coarse slaw, cover well with cold water, and let remain several hours before cooking, then drain and put into pot with enough boiling water to cover; boil on a Majestic Range until thoroughly cooked (which will generally require about forty-five minutes), add salt ten or fifteen minutes before removing from fire, and when done, take up in a colander, press out the water well, and season with butter and pepper. This is a good dish to serve with corned meats, but should not be cooked with them; if preferred, however, it may be seasoned by adding some of the liquor and fat from the boiling meat to the cabbage while cooking. Or, cut the cabbage in two, remove the hard stock, let stand in cold water two hours, tie in thin netting or piece of muslin, and boil in salted water for a longer time than when it is cut finely. Drain, remove, and serve in a dish with drawn butter, or a cream dressing poured over it.

GAS RANGES.

On the three following pages will be found cuts of our new line of Majestic Gas Ranges, with description. In the construction, bringing out, and introduction of these ranges we followed the dictates of a comprehensive understanding as to the wants of the people, and submit our work to their judgment.

It is not our policy to claim merit by decrying the make of others, hence we speak only of the Majestic. It may be difficult, but people will learn that a Gas Range should not be a temporary affair, used to-day, thrown away to-morrow. Judgment and sound sense ought to teach them that iron or steel subject to intense heat should be heavy, strong and well made.

The steady growth in the use of gas as a fuel for cooking induced us to undertake the manufacture of a Gas Range that would be permanent, in fact everlasting; and to this end we make them only of the best material obtainable.

The bodies, ovens, and centre flues are made of the best cold-rolled steel; oven doors, frames, hinges, stakes, and gravity handles, of malleable iron; other parts best gray iron. All parts in steel and malleable are riveted firmly and solidly together.

Our new Mantel and Closet Shelves are conveniences much appreciated by users. Our burners are new and made with a view to the smallest consumption of gas.

Our water heater is the largest ever made, it having 432 square inches of direct fire surface; it can be connected with either range. Our connecting gas pipes and pin valves are so made as to preclude the possibility of escaping gas, and are so simple that a child may connect and operate them.

Door panels and all fittings are nickel plated and highly polished. Shelf bands and brackets polished. Looked at from all the different standpoints, it is the greatest and best Gas Range in the world.

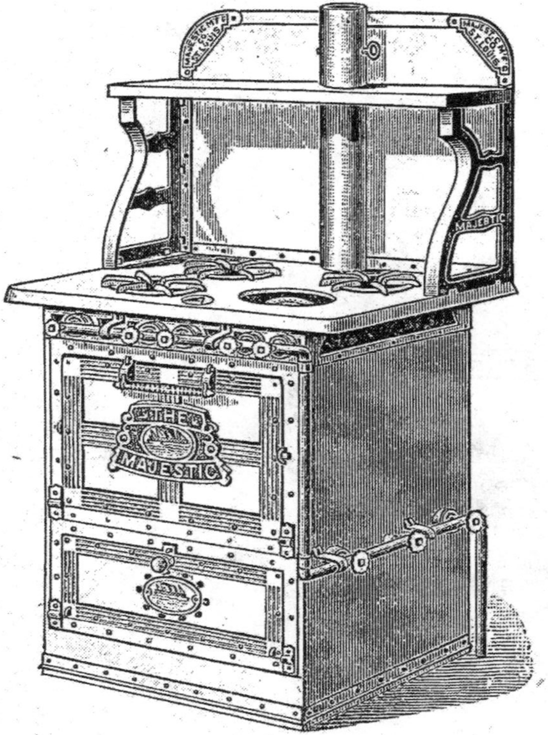

MAJESTIC GAS RANGE "A."

Has baking oven 16x18 in., 12½ in. high, 18 in. deep; broiling and toasting oven same width and depth by 8 in. high. Top surface 24x28 in., three single burners, one double, two oven burners, with automatic lighter, center flues, mantel shelf. The air mixers are provided with brass cut-offs, enabling the user to admit more or less air as suited to the variableness of gas and

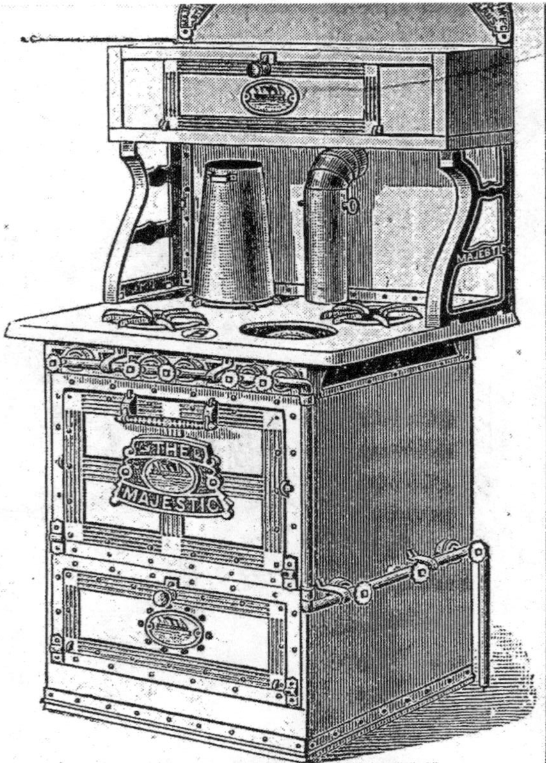

MAJESTIC GAS RANGE "B."

Is the same as range "A," except in place of single shelf it has our large warming oven, which is warmed by back burner on range, the heat being conveyed through a Russia iron hollow cone, placed over burner as shown, through which any desired temperature in warming oven may be obtained. When not in use the cone can be removed and hung to end of range. Cooks and belated guests thank us for this practical addition

Prices include delivery on board cars in St. Louis. Freight must be paid by purchasers—the rate varyi according to distance—from 25c to $2.00 per 100 lbs.

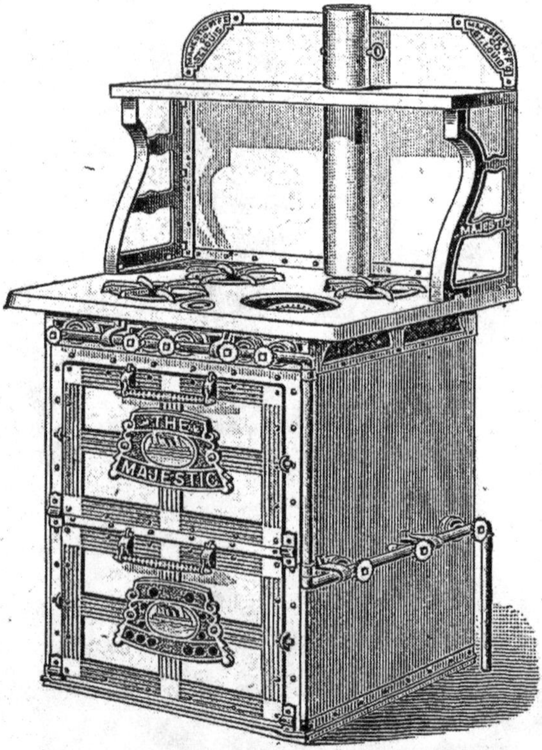

MAJESTIC GAS RANGE "C"

Has roasting and baking ovens, each 16 inches wide, 18 inches deep, 12½ inches high; top cooking surface 24x28 inches, and mantel shelf, three single burners, one double. The ovens are surrounded by double steel flues, and are heated by inverted twin burners producing a flame incandesent, thus enconomizing gas and utilizing to the fullest extent the products of the most perfect combustion ever produced in a gas range. Oven burners are lighted from the outside by needle lighter. For material and general constructive feature see page 11.

Price, $37.00.

Prices include delivery on board cars in St. Louis. Freight must be paid by purchasers—the rate varying according to distance—from 25c to $2.00 per 100 lbs.

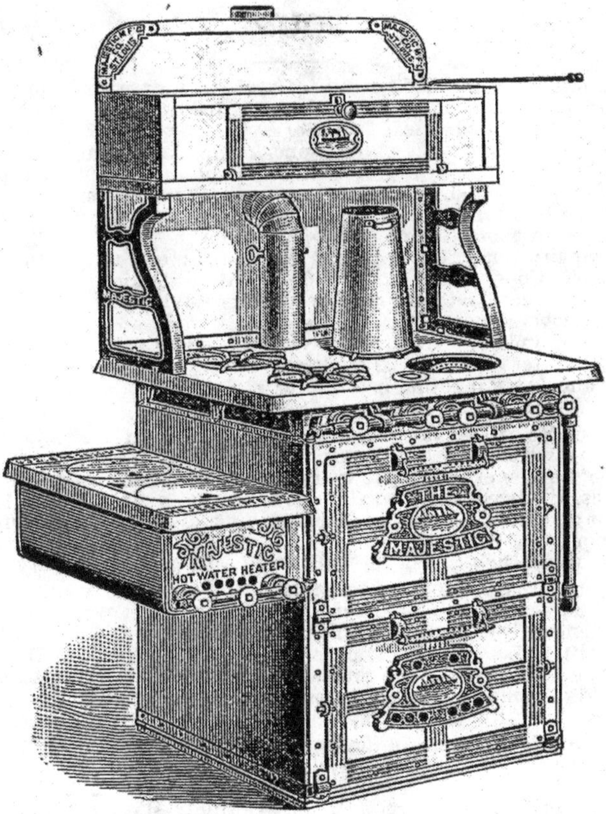

MAJESTIC GAS RANGE "D"

Is identically the same as Range "C" with our closet shelf and water heater connected. Air mixers, valves, cut-offs, burners and connections are the same on all.

This range is complete in all its details, and will do cooking and heat water for ten to fifteen persons.

Price, $50.00.

Prices include delivery on board cars in St. Louis. Freight must be paid by purchasers—the rate varying according to distance—from 25c to $2.00 per 100 lbs.

SOUPS.

Stock.—Four pounds of shin of beef, or four pounds of knuckle of veal, or two pounds of each; any bones, trimmings of poultry, or fresh meat, quarter pound of lean bacon or ham, two ounces of butter, two large onions, each stuck with cloves; one turnip, three carrots, one head of celery, three lumps of sugar, two ounces of salt, half a teaspoonful of whole pepper, one large blade of mace, one bunch of savory herbs, four quarts and half pint of cold water. Cut up the meat and bacon, or ham, into pieces of about three inches square; rub the butter on the bottom of the stewpan; put in half a pint of water, the meat, and all the other ingredients. Cover the stewpan, and place it on a Majestic Range, having a sharp fire, occasionally stirring its contents. When the bottom of the pan becomes covered with a pale, jelly-like substance, add the four quarts of cold water, and simmer very gently for five hours. As we have said before, do not let it boil quickly. Remove every particle of scum while it is doing, and strain it through a five hair sieve. Time: five and one half hours. Average cost, twenty-five cents per quart.

Beef Soup.—Take bones and trimmings from a sirloin steak, put over fire after breakfast in three quarts water, boil steadily until about an hour before dinner, when add two onions, one carrot, three common-sized potatoes, all sliced, some parsley cut fine, a red pepper, and salt to taste and put on a Majestic Range. This makes a delicious soup, sufficient for three persons. All soups are more palatable seasoned with onions and red pepper, using the seeds of the latter with care, as they are very strong.

Veal Soup.—To about three pounds of a joint of veal, which must be well broken up, put four quarts of water and set it over to boil on a Majestic Range. Prepare one fourth pound of macaroni by boiling it by itself, with sufficient water to cover it; add a little butter to the macaroni when it is tender, strain the soup and season to taste with salt and pepper, then add the macaroni in the water in which it is boiled. The addition of a pint of rich milk or cream and celery flavor is relished by many.

Chicken Soup.—In boiling chickens for salad, etc., the broth (water in which they are boiled) may be used for soup. When the chickens are to be served whole, stuff and tie in a cloth. To the broth add a dozen tomatoes (or a quart can), and one thinly-sliced onion; boil twenty minutes on a Majestic Range, season with salt and pepper, add two well-beaten eggs and serve.

Noodles for Soup.—Rub into two eggs as much sifted flour as they will absorb; then roll out until thin as a wafer; dust over a little flour, and then roll over and over into a roll, cut off thin slices from the edge of the roll and shake out into long strips; put them into the soup lightly and boil for ten minutes on a Majestic Range; salt should be added while mixing with the flour—about a saltspoonful.

Oyster Soup.—Two quarts of oysters, one quart of milk, two tablespoonfuls of butter, one teacupful hot water; pepper, salt. Strain all the liquor from the oysters; add the water and heat. When near the boil, add the seasoning, then the oysters. Cook on a Majestic Range about five minutes from the time they begin to simmer, until they "ruffle." Stir in the butter, cook one minute and pour into the tureen. Stir in the boiling milk, and send to table.

Tomato Soup.—Tomato soup is a much relished American dish, and is prepared as follows: Steam, or rather stew slowly, a mess of turnips, carrots, and onions, also a stalk of celery, with half a pound of lean ham and a *little bit* of fresh butter over a slow fire for an hour or so on a Majestic Range. Then add two quarts of diluted stock or of other liquor in which meat has been boiled, as also eight or ten ripe tomatoes. Stew the whole for an hour and a half, then pass through the sieve into the pan again; add a little pepper and salt, boil for ten minutes and serve hot.

To Get up a Soup in Haste.—Chop some cold cooked meat fine, and put a pint into a stew-pan with some gravy, season with pepper and salt and a little butter if the gravy is not rich, add a little flour moistened with cold water, and three pints boiling water, boiled moderately half an hour on a Majestic Range. Strain over some rice or nicely toasted bread, and serve. Uncooked meat may be used by using one quart of cold water to a pound of chopped meat, and letting it stand half an hour before boiling. Celery root may be grated in as seasoning, or a bunch of parsley thrown in.

Bean Soup.—Boil a small soup-bone in about two quarts water until the meat can be separated from the bone, remove bone, add a coffee-cup white beans soaked for two hours, boil for an hour and a half on a Majestic Range, add three potatoes, half a turnip and a parsnip, all sliced fine, boil half an hour longer, and just before serving sprinkle in a few dry bread-crumbs; season with salt and pepper, and serve with raw onions sliced very fine for those who like them.

Potato Soup.—Potato soup is suitable for a cold day. Make it in the following manner: Get as many beef or ham bones as you can, and smash them into fragments. Add a little bit of lean ham to give flavor. Boil the bone and ham for two hours and a half at least on a Majestic Range. The bone of a roast beef is excellent. Strain off the liquor carefully, empty out the bones and *debris* of the ham, restore the liquor to the pot, and place again on the fire. Having selected, washed, and pared some nice potatoes, cut them into small pieces, and boil them in the stock till they melt away. An onion or two may also be boiled among the bones to help the flavor. I do not like thick potato soup, and I usually strain it through a hair sieve, after doing so placing it again on the fire, seasoning it with pepper and salt to taste. A stick of celery boiled with the bones is an improvement. Make only the quantity required for the day, as potato soup is best when it is newly made.

Ox-Tail Soup.—Take two ox tails and two whole onions, two carrots, a small turnip, two tablespoonfuls of flour, and a little white pepper, add a gallon of water, let all boil for two hours on a Majestic Range; then take out the tails and cut the meat into small pieces, return the bones to the pot, for a short time, boil for another hour, then strain the soup, and rinse two spoonfuls of arrowroot to add to it with the meat cut from the bones, and let all boil for a quarter of an hour.

Vegetable Soup.—Two pounds of course, lean beef, cut into strips, two pounds of knuckle of veal, chopped to pieces, two pounds of mutton bones, and the bones left from your cold veal, cracked to splinters, one pound of lean ham, four large carrots, two turnips, two onions, bunch of herbs, three tablespoonfuls of butter, and two of flour, one tablespoonful of sugar, salt and pepper, seven quarts of water. Put on meat, bones, herbs and water, and cook slowly five hours on a Majestic Range. Strain the soup, of which there should be five quarts. Season meat and bones, and put into the stock-pot with three quarts of the liquor. Save this for days to come. While the soup for to-day is cooling that you may take off the fat, put the butter into a frying pan with the sliced carrots, turnips, and onions, and fry to a light brown. Now, add a pint of the skimmed stock, and stew the vegetables tender, stir in the flour wet with water, and put all, with your cooled stock, over the fire in the soup-kettle. Season with sugar, cayenne and salt, boil five minutes, rub through a colander, then a soup-sieve, heat almost to boiling, and serve.

Lobster Soup.—Procure a large hen fish, boiled, and with all its coral, if possible. Cut away from it all the meat in neat little pieces; beat up the fins and minor claws in a mortar, then stew the results in a stew-pan, slowly, along with a little white stock; season this with a bunch of sweet herbs; a small onion, a little bit of celery, and a carrot may be placed in the stock, as also the toasted crust of a French roll. Season to taste with salt and a little cayenne. Simmer the whole for about an hour on a Majestic Range; then strain and return the liquor to the saucepan, place in it the pieces of lobster, and having beaten up the coral in a little flour and gravy, stir it in. Let the soup remain on the fire for a few minutes without boiling and serve hot. A small strip of the rind of a lemon may be boiled in the stock, and a little nutmeg may be added to the seasoning. This is a troublesome soup to prepare, but there are many who like it when it is well made.

Green Pea Soup.—Wash a small quarter of lamb in cold water, and put it into a soup-pot with six quarts of cold water; add to it two tablespoonfuls of salt, and set it on a Majestic Range over a moderate fire —let it boil gently for two hours, then skim it clear, add a quart of shelled peas, and a teaspoonful of pepper; cover it, and let it boil for half an hour, then having scraped the skins from a quart of small young potatoes, add them to the soup; cover the pot, and let it boil for half an hour longer; work quarter pound of butter, and a dessert spoonful of flour together, and add them to the soup ten or twelve minutes before taking it off the fire. Serve the meat on the dish with parsley sauce over, and the soup in a tureen.

OYSTERS.

Escaloped Oysters.—Take crushed crackers not too fine; drain liquor from a quart of oysters and carefully remove all bits of shell; butter a deep dish or pan, cover the bottom with crackers, put in a layer of oysters seasoned with salt and pepper and bits of butter in plenty, then a layer of crackers, then oysters, and so on until dish is full, finishing with the crackers covered with bits of butter; pour over the whole the oyster liquor added to one pint of boiling water (boiled and skimmed), place in a hot Majestic Range oven, bake half an hour, add another pint of hot water, or half pint water and half pint of milk, in which a small lump of butter has been melted; bake another half hour, and, to prevent browning too much, cover with a tin or sheet iron lid. All bread-crumbs, or a mixture of crackers and bread-crumbs may be used when more convenient. As the amount of liquor in oysters varies, and the proportion of crackers or bread-crumbs to the oysters also varies, the quantity of water must be increased or diminished according to judgment and taste. Some prefer to cook half the time given above. Boiled macaroni may be used in place of cracker crumbs.

Fried Oysters.—Drain carefully, remove all bits of shell, and sprinkle with pepper and salt, and set in a cool place for ten or fifteen minutes. Then, if oysters are small, pour them into a pan of crackers rolled fine, add the liquor, mix well, and let stand five minutes, add a little salt and pepper, mold into small cakes with two or three oysters in each, roll in dry crackers until well encrusted, and fry in a Majestic Range, in hot lard and butter, or beef-drippings. Serve hot in a covered dish.

Or, dip the oysters in the yolk of eggs, well seasoned and beaten, then in corn meal with a little baking powder mixed with it, and fry in Majestic Range, in hot lard like doughnuts; or if you have frying basket, place them on that and drop it in the hot lard. Test the heat as for doughnuts.

Or, drain thoroughly, put in a hot frying-pan, in a Majestic Range, turn so as to brown on both sides. They cook in this way in a few moments, and the peculiar flavor of the oysters is well preserved. Serve on a hot covered dish, with butter, pepper and salt, or add a little cream just before serving, and serve on toast; or take two parts rolled crackers and one part corn meal, mix well, roll the oysters in it, and fry in equal parts butter and lard. Season with salt and pepper.

Oyster Fritters.—Drain off liquor, boil, skim, and to a cupful add a cup of milk, two or three eggs, salt and pepper, and flour enough to make a rather thick batter. Have hot lard or beef drippings ready in a kettle, on a Majestic Range, drop the batter into it with a large spoon, taking up one oyster for each spoonful. The oyster must be large and plump.

Panned Oysters.—Cut stale bread in thin slices, then round them, removing all crust. Make them to fit patty-pans; toast them, butter, and place in pans. Moisten with three or four teaspoons of oyster liquor; then place on the toast a layer of oysters, sprinkle with pepper, and put on top a small piece of butter; place pans in a baking pan and put in a Majestic Range oven, covering with a tin lid, or if not large enough, another pan to keep in the steam and flavor; have a quick oven, and when cooked seven or eight minutes, until "ruffled," remove cover and sprinkle with salt; replace cover and cook one minute longer. Serve in the patty-pans. This is delicious.

Oyster Roll.—Cut a round piece, say six inches across, from the top of a well-baked round loaf of bread, remove the inside from the loaf, leaving crust half an inch thick; make a rich oyster stew, and put in the loaf first a layer of it, then of bread crumbs, then oysters, and so on; place cover over the top, glaze the loaf with the beaten yolk of an egg, and place in Majestic Range oven for a few moments. Serve very hot.

Oysters in the Shell.—Open the shells, keeping the deepest ones for use. Melt some butter, season with minced parsley and pepper. When slightly cooled, roll each oyster in it, using care that it drips but little, and lay in the shells. Add to each shell a little lemon juice, cover with grated bread-crumbs, place in a baking-pan and bake in a quick Majestic Range oven; just before they are done add a little salt. Serve in the shells.

Oyster Stew.—Put the liquor from the oysters on the Majestic Range, let boil, skim, and season with butter and pepper, add oysters, let come to a boil only, season with salt and serve. This is pronounced a "royal stew."

Steamed Oysters.—Lay some oysters in the shell in some air-tight vessel, placing the upper shell downward so the liquor will not run out when they open. Set them on a Majestic Range over a pot of boiling water (where they will get the steam), and boil hard for twenty minutes; if the oysters are open they are done; if not, steam till they do open. Serve at once and eat hot, with salt and a bit of butter.

Or, wash and drain one quart select oysters, put on a Majestic Range, in pan, and place in steamer over boiling water, cover and steam till oysters are plump with edges ruffled; place in heated dish with butter, pepper and salt, and serve.

Oyster Omelet.—Add to a half cup of cream six eggs beaten very light, season with pepper and salt, pour into a frying-pan on a Majestic Range, with a tablespoon of butter; drop in a dozen large oysters cut in halves, or chopped fine with parsely, and fry until a light brown. Double it over and serve immediately.

Oyster Patties.—Take of oysters according to the number to be served. Place the oysters in the same pan with butter, pepper, salt and a little flour; stir, and let simmer a few minutes on a Majestic Range. Bake shells of rich puff paste in patty tins, and also small rounds for covers; heat the shells and fill with oysters; put on the covers and set in the Majestic Range oven for five minutes. Serve immediately.

PUDDINGS.

Christmas Plum Pudding.—One pound of suet, chopped fine, one pound of sugar, one pound of grated bread, one pound of raisins, two pounds of currants, one glass of brandy, two teaspoonfuls of ground ginger, two teaspoonfuls of nutmeg, one of cloves, a pinch of salt, one pint of milk; beat well, and steam five hours on a Majestic Range. Serve with rich wine sauce.

Fruit Pudding.—One cup of suet, chopped; one cup of molasses, one cup of brown sugar, one cup of milk, three cups of flour, one teaspoonful of cloves, one tablespoonful of baking powder, one cup of chopped raisins; steam three hours on a Majestic Range. Serve with sauce.

Suet Pudding.—One cup of suet, one of molasses. one cup of milk, one cup of seeded raisins, two cups of Graham flour, one cup of wheat flour, one teaspoonful of baking powder. Steam three hours on a Majestic Range.

Graham Pudding.—Two cups of Graham flour, one cup of molasses, one-half cup of milk, one cup of raisins, one pinch of salt, and one teaspoonful of soda. Steam two hours on a Majestic Range.

Puff Pudding.—Mix one pint of flour, one teaspoonful of baking powder, a pinch of salt, and milk enough to make a batter. Pour into a greased pan; put steamed apples on top, then pour on more batter. Steam one-half hour on a Majestic Range. Serve with hard sauce.

Queen of Puddings.—One pint of bread crumbs, one quart of milk, one cup of sugar, yolks of four eggs, one tablespoonful of butter, one teaspoonful extract of lemon. Bake in a Majestic Range; spread with a layer of fruit jelly. Whip the whites of the eggs to a froth with one cup of sugar and the juice of one lemon; then spread on top and brown.

Cream Pudding.—Mix one-half cup of sugar and one grated lemon. Beat six eggs to a froth, and add one pint of flour, one pint of milk and one pint of rich cream, a pinch of salt. Bake in a buttered dish in a Majestic Range. Serve with lemon sauce.

Tipsy Pudding.—Saturate a loaf of sponge cake, baked in a Majestic Range, with wine or brandy; make a rich boiled custard, place the cake in a deep glass dish, and pour the custard over it. Stick the top full of blanched almonds, and serve cold.

Rice Pudding.—One quart of milk, four eggs, one-half cup of rice, three-quarters cup of sugar, one tablespoonful of butter, one-half cup of raisins, seeded and chopped; boil the rice five minutes in one pint of milk. When cool, add the yolks of the eggs, also butter and sugar, then the pint of unboiled milk, the whites of the eggs and the raisins last; add one teaspoonful of nutmeg. Cook one hour on a Majestic Range, and eat cold.

Orange Pudding.—Peel and cut up six oranges into the bottom of a dish; pour over them a custard. Make the frosting of the whites of four eggs and one-third of a cup of sugar. Spread over the top, brown a little in a Majestic Range and serve cold.

Chocolate Pudding.—One pint of milk, one pint of bread crumbs, yolks of three eggs, five tablespoonfuls of grated chocolate; scald the milk, and add bread crumbs and chocolate, take from the fire and add one-half cup of sugar and the yolks of three eggs; bake fifteen minutes in a Majestic Range. Spread wilh meringue, brown, and serve with cream.

Cottage Pudding.—One cup of milk, one-half cup of sugar, one egg, one tablespoonful of melted butter, two tablespoonfuls of baking powder; flavor with extract of lemon; bake one-half hour in a Majestic Range. Serve with lemon sauce.

Railroad Pudding.—Beat one egg, add one cup of sugar, one teaspoonful of melted butter, one and one-half cups of flour, one teaspoonful of baking powder, one-half cup of milk, one teaspoonful extract of lemon; bake in a Majestic Range. Serve with foaming sauce.

Peach Cottage Pudding.—Stir sliced peaches into a batter made of one-half cup of sugar, three tablespoonfuls of melted butter, one beaten egg, one cup of milk, one pint of flour. three teaspoonfuls of baking powder; bake in a loaf in a Majestic Range, Serve with hard sauce.

Tapioca Fruit Pudding.—Soak one cup of tapioca over night, cook soft in water, then add, and cook thoroughly on a Majestic Range, one pint preserved raspberries, cool in a mold; serve with sugar and cream.

Chocolate Pudding No. 2.—Boil one pint of milk, add one-half cup of sugar, two tablespoonfuls of grated chocolate, one large spoonful of corn starch; boil on a Majestic Range until thickened, then pour into a mould and place on ice. Serve with cream flavored with extract of vanilla.

Macaroni Pudding.—One cup broken macaroni, one quart milk, four eggs, juice and grated peel of one-half lemon, three-quarters of a cup of sugar and two tablespoonfuls of butter; boil the macaroni in one-half the milk until tender; while hot stir in the butter, sugar, lemon and eggs. Bake in a buttered mould one-half hour in a Majestic Range.

Delmonico Pudding.—One quart of milk, one tablespoonful of corn starch dissolved in cold milk; yolks of five eggs well beaten, six tablespoonfuls of sugar; boil five minutes, then pour into a pudding dish and bake one hour in a Majestic Range; beat the whites of six eggs with sugar and flavor with extract of lemon; return to the Majestic oven and brown.

Indian Pudding.—Pour enough boiling water on two cups of Indian meal to wet, add one-half cup of butter, one cup of sugar, a pinch of salt, two cups of milk, one-half cup of molasses and one cup of seeded raisins; one teaspoonful extract of cinnamon and a little nutmeg. Bake three hours in a Majestic Range, and serve with cream.

COFFEE, TEA, ETC.

Steamed Coffee.—Put coffee into the pot, pour the boiling water on it; place this pot (which is made to fit) into the top of the tea-kettle, and let cook from ten to twenty minutes on a Majestic Range, while water in kettle is kept boiling all the time. This makes a clear, delicious coffee. Some persons hold that by first wetting the coffee with cold water, bringing it to boiling point, and then pouring in water, more of the strength is extracted.

Army Coffee.—Coffee or tea may be made quickly by placing the required quantity of cold water in the pot and adding the coffee tied up in a sack of a fine gauze or piece of muslin; bring to boiling point, boil five minutes and serve. Make tea in the same way, except that the tea is put loose in the water and simply allowed to boil up once on a Majestic Range.

Coffee with Whipped Cream.—For six cups of coffee of fair size take one cup sweet cream whipped light with a little sugar; put into each cup the desired amount of sugar and about a tablespoon boiling milk; pour the coffee over these and lay upon the surface of the hot liquid a large spoonful of the frothed cream, giving a gentle stir to each cup before serving. This is known to some as meringued coffee and is an elegant French preparation of the popular drink. Chocolate served in this way is delicious.

Vienna Coffee.—Filter instead of boiling the coffee, allowing one tablespoon ground coffee to each person and "one for the pot;" put a quart of cream into a custard kettle or pail set in boiling water, and put it where it will keep boiling; beat the white of an egg to a froth, and mix well with three tablespoons cold milk. As soon as the cream is hot remove from fire, add the mixed egg and milk, stir together briskly for a minute, and then serve.

Another method is to pour boiling water over the coffee, cover closely, boil one minute, remove to the side of the range a few minutes to settle, and serve. Allow two heaping tablespoons coffee to a pint of water. The less time the coffee is cooked the more coffee is required, but the finer the flavor. The late Professor Blot protested against boiling the coffee at all, as in his opinion the aroma was evaporated and only the bitter flavor left.

Tea.—Pour into a granite tea-steeper a very little boiling water, and then put in the tea, allowing one teaspoon of tea to each person. Pour over this boiling water until the steeper is little more than half full; cover tightly and let it stand where it will keep hot but not boil. Let the tea infuse, for ten or fifteen minutes and then pour into the granite tea-urn, adding more boiling water, in the proportion of one cup of water for every teaspoon of dry tea which has been infused. Have boiling water in a water-pot, and weaken each cup of tea as desired. Do not use water for tea that has boiled long. Spring water is best for tea, and filtered water next best. Tea should never be boiled, but be sure that the water boils that you use for steeping. From three to five minutes is sufficient time; if it stands longer the tea is apt to lose its aroma and have the bitter taste of the leaf.

Chocolate.—Grate chocolate, allowing for one quart of water six tablespoonfuls of chocolate; mix smooth with a little water and boil fifteen minutes on a Majestic Range, add one quart rich milk, boil a few minutes longer, and serve hot, with sugar.

Chocolate.—Take six tablespoons scraped chocolate, or three of chocolate and three of cocoa, dissolve in a quart of boiling water, boil hard fifteen minutes, add one quart of rich milk, let scald, and serve hot. This is enough for six persons. Cocoa can also be made after this recipe: Some boil either coca or chocolate only one minute and then serve, while others make it the day before using, boiling it for one hour on a Majestic Range, and when cool skimming off the oil, and when wanted for use, heat it to the boiling point and add the milk. In this way it is equally good and much more wholesome. Cocoa is from the seed of the fruit of a small tropical tree. There are several forms in which it is sold, the most nutritious and convenient being chocolate, the next cocoa, then cocoa nibs, and last cocoa shells. The ground bean is simply cocoa; ground fine and mixed with sugar it is chocolate; the beans broken into bits are "nibs." The shells are the shells of the bean, usually removed before grinding. The beans are roasted like coffee and ground between hot rollers.

Vienna Chocolate.—Put into a coffee-pot set in boiling water one quart of new milk (or a pint each of cream and milk), stir into it three heaping tablespoons grated chocolate mixed to a paste with a cold milk, let it boil two or three minutes and serve at once. To make good chocolate good materials are required.

Iced Tea.—Prepare tea in the morning making it stronger and sweeter than usual; strain and pour into a clean stone jug or glass bottle and set aside in the ice-chest until ready to use. Drink from goblets without cream. Serve ice broken in small pieces on a platter nicely garnished with well-washed grape leaves. Iced tea may be prepared from either green or black alone, but it is considered an improvement to mix the two. Tea made like that for iced tea (or that left in the tea-pot after a meal), with sugar to taste, a slice or two of lemon, a little of the juice, and some pieces of cracked ice makes a delightful drink. Serve in glasses.

WHAT PEOPLE SHOULD KNOW.

That a range, a stove, or heating apparatus, has no more draught than a steam boiler or a square box.

That the chimney creates the draught; the taller, the better the draught.

That it should be higher than any other part of the building.

That it should be not less than 9x9 inches inside, and smooth.

That two smoke pipes should not enter the same chimney.

That every other flue opening in the chimney must be closed.

That the space below where the pipe enters should be cut off

That new chimneys are often left half filled with brick and mortar.

That old flues are often cracked outside, not half high enough, and full of soot.

That such conditions kill the draught.

That the pipe entering chimney must be same size as on the range.

That the larger the range, the larger and higher must be the chimney.

That good fuel must be provided; if wood, well seasoned; if coal, well selected.

That the fire-box should not be filled above top of linings.

That the flues of range must be cleaned once a week.

That in 10,000 Majestic Ranges not twenty complaints are made by the users.

That such complaints are caused wholly by bad flues, or inefficient cooks.

That our guarantee is based upon the assumption

That the purchaser will provide the proper chimney flue.

That dealers are not authorized to say—"They will take it back."

That it is too well established to need such an assertion.

That we and our dealers guarantee the range, and not the flue.

That under proper conditions nothing on earth works better.

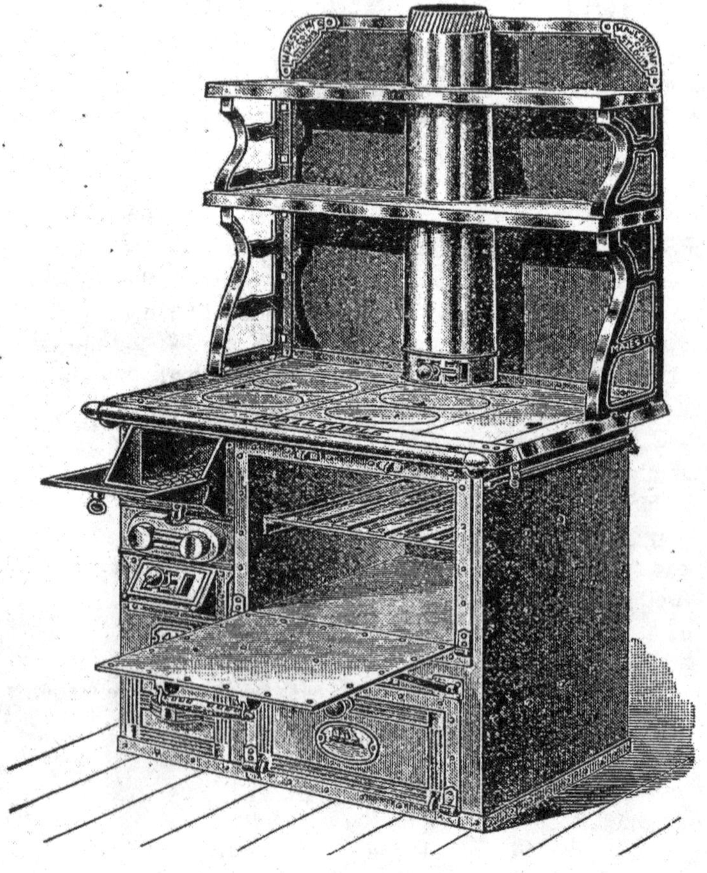

MAJESTIC RANGE A.

For Double Mantel Shelf when taken IN PLACE of plain we charge extra, $2.00.

SEE PAGE 9.

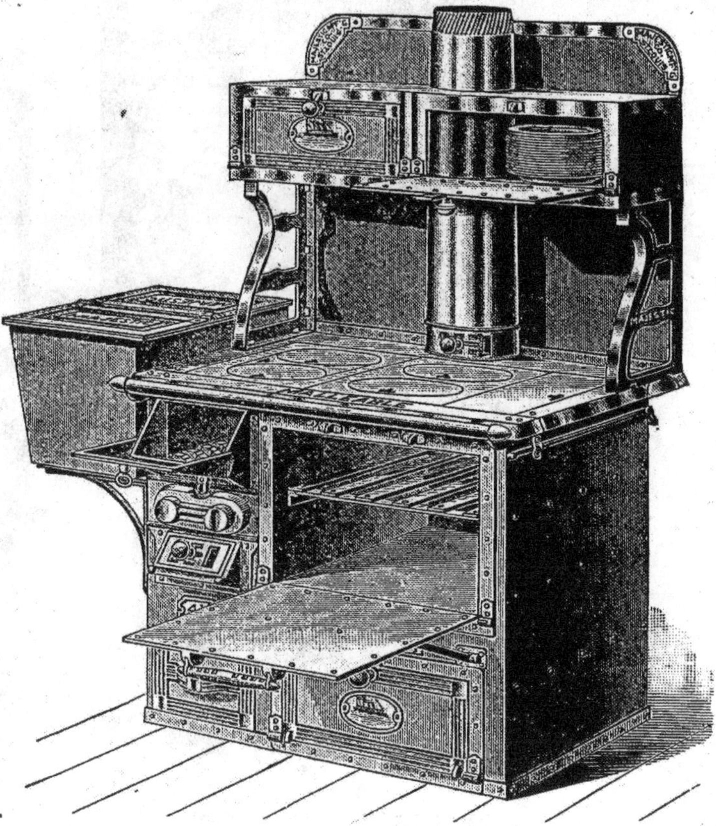

MAJESTIC RANGE B.

For Double Closet Shelf when taken IN PLACE of plain we charge extra, $5.00.

SEE PAGE 9.

MAJESTIC RANGE C.

Charcoal Broiler connected, - - - -	extra,	$10.00.
40-gallon Galvanized Iron Pressure Boiler connected, -	extra,	21.00.
Double Closet Shelf IN PLACE of plain, - -	extra,	5.00.

Broiler or Boiler may be connected on either end of Range, as desired.

SEE PAGE 9.

CIRCULATING BOILER.

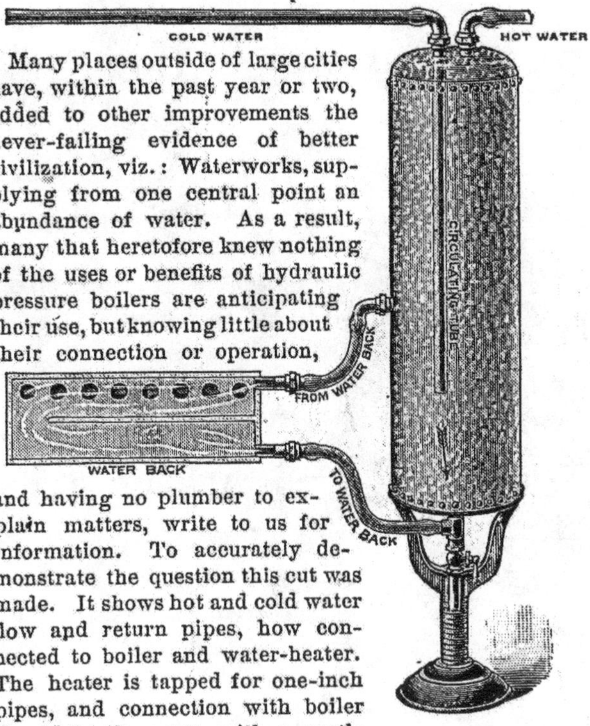

Many places outside of large cities have, within the past year or two, added to other improvements the never-failing evidence of better civilization, viz.: Waterworks, supplying from one central point an abundance of water. As a result, many that heretofore knew nothing of the uses or benefits of hydraulic pressure boilers are anticipating their use, but knowing little about their connection or operation, and having no plumber to explain matters, write to us for information. To accurately demonstrate the question this cut was made. It shows hot and cold water flow and return pipes, how connected to boiler and water-heater. The heater is tapped for one-inch pipes, and connection with boiler should be the same, with a gentle easy curve, as shown in cut. Short angles greatly retard circulation.

Open. Closed.

NEW REGULATING DAMPERS.

This illustration shows our New Regulating Dampers, which are used on all Hotel Ranges with two ovens, one fire. The simplicity of this invention recommends it to all users, as there is nothing to get out of repair, and a child can operate it. The cut explains itself.

CPSIA information can be obtained
at www.ICGtesting.com
Printed in the USA
JSHW051814230222
23255JS00001B/40

9 781429 011150